Zaha Hadid — LF one

Zaha Hadid with P. Schumacher, M. Dochantschi
and mayer bährle

LF one

Landscape Formation one in Weil am Rhein, Germany
With photographs by / Mit Photographien von
Christian Richters

Birkhäuser Publishers
Basel · Boston · Berlin

Supported by / Unterstützt durch: Landesgartenschau Weil am Rhein 1999 GmbH

Translation into English / Übersetzung ins Englische: Katja Steiner, Bruce Almberg, Ehingen
Layout / Gestaltung: Office of Zaha Hadid (Dochantschi, Hof), mayer bährle

A CIP catalogue record for this book is available from the Library of Congress, Washington D.C., USA.

Die Deutsche Bibliothek – Cataloging-in-Publication Data

Hadid, Zaha:
LF one : landscape formation Weil am Rhein / Zaha M. Hadid.
[Transl. German into Engl.: Katja Steiner ; Bruce Almberg]. – Basel ; Boston ; Berlin : Birkhäuser, 1999
ISBN 3-7643-6029-1 (Basel ...)
ISBN 0-8176-6029-1 (Boston ...)

This work is subject to copyright. All rights are reserved, whether the whole or part of the material is concerned, specifically the rights of translation, reprinting, re-use of illustrations, recitation, broadcasting, reproduction on microfilms or in other ways, and storage in data banks.
For any kind of use permission of the copyright owner must be obtained.

© 1999 Birkhäuser – Publishers for Architecture, P.O. Box 133, CH-4010 Basel, Switzerland.
Printed on acid-free paper produced of chlorine-free pulp. TCF ∞
Printed in Germany
ISBN 3-7643-6029-1
ISBN 0-8176-6029-1

9 8 7 6 5 4 3 2 1

Contents / Inhaltsverzeichnis

Introduction / Einleitung 7
Klaus Eberhardt

LF one, Weil am Rhein 17
Natural and Artificial Landscape Formations /
Natürliche und künstliche Landschaftsformationen
Office Zaha Hadid

Thoughts on the essence of being 1–3 / Gedanken zum Sosein 1–3 59
mayer bährle

The Perfection of Modernism / Die Vollendung der Moderne 77
Michael Mönninger

Promenade architecturale 87
Christian Richters

Biographies / Biographien 104
Project Data / Projektdaten 107
Illustration Credits / Bildnachweis 108

Introduction

"Even the most beautiful place in nature is not yet a garden, no matter how enchanting we may find it. It only becomes a garden if we form it with our own hands and fill it with our dreams."

(Charles W. Moore, William J. Mitchell, William Turnbull jr., *The Poetics of Gardens*)

I. The Park Concept for Weil am Rhein

Places can be read like faces, said the old Romans. Every place – just like every person – has its individual genius which, when observed, reveals itself as a kind of soul.

The property intended for a new park in Weil am Rhein in an open gravel quarry, which was to be designed for the occasion of the gardening show 1999, offered an unusually exciting backdrop for the poetic reinterpretation of a "second" natural landscape. In this new, artificially created "gravel" landscape, the traditional categories of artificiality and naturalness, or culture and nature, no longer apply. The newly created spectrum of landscaped spaces, ground formations and plant communities offers fascinating preconditions for a new park interpretation, for artificial designs and individual interventions in an environment of a wild plant population with many species. What is debatable as a conceptual idea is not the ecologically influenced renaturalization or even the reestablishment of a former landscape but

Einleitung

«Selbst der schönste Platz in der Natur ist noch kein Garten, wie bezaubernd wir ihn auch finden. Zum Garten wird er erst, wenn wir ihn mit eigenen Händen formen und mit unseren Träumen erfüllen.»

(Charles W. Moore, William J. Mitchell, William Turnbull jr., The Poetics of Gardens)

I. Das Parkkonzept für Weil am Rhein

Orte lassen sich lesen wie Gesichter, sagten die Römer. Jeder Ort – wie jeder Mensch – besaß für sie einen individuellen Genius, der sich beim Betrachten als eine Art Seele offenbarte.

Das für einen neuen Park in Weil am Rhein vorgesehene Gelände in einer aufgelassenen Kiesgrube, die im Zuge der Landesgartenschau 1999 gestaltet werden sollte, bot eine außergewöhnlich spannende Kulisse für die poesievolle Neuinterpretation einer «zweiten» Naturlandschaft. In dieser artifiziell geschaffenen neuen Kunstlandschaft «Kies» stimmen die tradierten Kategorien von Künstlichkeit und Natürlichkeit – oder Kultur und Natur – nicht mehr. Das neu entstandene Spektrum von Landschaftsräumen, Geländeformationen, Pflanzengemeinschaften bietet faszinierende Voraussetzungen für eine neue Parkinterpretation, für artifizielle Gestaltungen und einzelne Interventionen in einer Umgebung von artenreichen, wilden Pflanzenbeständen. Nicht die ökologisch geprägte Renaturierung oder gar die Wiederherstellung einer ehemaligen Landschaft stehen als Konzeptidee zur Debatte, sondern intelligente Verfremdungen die-

Aerial view LF one site, 1995
Luftbild Gelände LF one, 1995

rather the thoughtful alienation of this new landscape with traces of history and artistic interventions, an excitingly staged plant world in harmony with the ecology! With the stage sets that offer themselves for this almost archaic natural space with the landscape-related, urban and architectural special features of the city of Weil, a genius loci of a park can be developed that will stand out in a pleasing way from the contextual leitmotif of an international gardening show – a bit of everything, nicely mixed, flowering voluptuously, uncomplicated in its design and ecologically appealing.

II. Urban and Industrial Culture

After decades of influence by buildings and the railroad system on the image of the city of Weil am Rhein, a new corporate identity of the city was able to be gained through the new world architecture of Frank O. Gehry (Vitra Design Museum), Zaha M. Hadid (the Vitra fire station appliance building), Tadao Ando (the Vitra conference building) and the unusual production halls by Frank O. Gehry, Nicholas Grimshaw and Alvaro Siza.

The manager of the Vitra conglomerate, Dr Rolf Fehlbaum, no longer saw the relationship with the city on an administrative level; he now experienced his architectural park as a part of the city in two respects: first, as a spectacular city entrance, replacing the former perimeter

ser neuen Landschaft mit Spuren der Geschichte, mit künstlerischen Interventionen, mit einer spannungsvoll inszenierten Pflanzenwelt im Einklang mit der Ökologie! Dank der sich anbietenden Inszenierungen dieses fast archaisch anmutenden Naturraumes mit den landschaftlichen, städtebaulichen und architektonischen Besonderheiten der Stadt Weil am Rhein läßt sich ein Genius loci eines Parkes entwickeln, der sich von den inhaltlichen Leitmotiven einer üblichen Landesgartenschau – von allem etwas, schön gemischt, üppig blühend, gestalterisch unkompliziert, ökologisch ansprechend usw. – angenehm abheben wird.

II. Stadt und Industriekultur

Jahrzehntelang wurde das Image der Stadt Weil am Rhein wesentlich durch Bauten und Anlagen der Eisenbahn geprägt. Mit den neuen bedeutenden Architekturen von Frank O. Gehry (Vitra Design Museum), Zaha M. Hadid (Feuerwehrgerätehaus Vitra), Tadao Ando (Konferenzgebäude Vitra) sowie den aussergewöhnlichen Vitra-Produktionshallen von Frank O. Gehry, Nicholas Grimshaw und Alvaro Siza vollzog sich eine erfreuliche Erneuerung der Corporate identity der Stadt.

Der Leiter der Vitra-Firmen, Dr. Rolf Fehlbaum, sah die Beziehungen zur Stadt nicht mehr auf einer nur administrativen Ebene, sondern er erfuhr nunmehr seinen Architekturpark als Teil der Stadt – und dies in zweierlei Hinsicht: einerseits als spektakulärer Stadteingang anstelle der früheren Randlage, ande-

Aerial view, Vitra
Luftbild, Vitra

situation, and second, as an important contribution to the overall urban culture. The realization of a common building forum for establishing a commonly developed urban concept in the sense of a public/private partnership initiated project ideas and planning visions that were not just directed towards the synergetic interactions of industry and urban development but that also influenced the network of relations between the city and the landscape.

While Frank O. Gehry demanded the reintegration of the Rhine River into the urban organism, Zaha M. Hadid's designs stood out through their exaggeration of typical landscape structures into the adjoining building structures of the city. By taking up the theme of the almost corridor-shaped landscape structures into the development areas, the city itself became an artificial landscape in the case of the Vitra complex.

In the workshop by the city and Vitra, an additional perspective by Alessandro Mendini was also opened up: "We have to look at a city not only as a materialization of the planned but also as a materialization of the atmospheric." He suggests routes through the city that also open up to the individual the sensual and poetic. The basic concept of a connection – no matter how – of perceivable stations was thus created and with it the connection between the new urban culture around Vitra and the cultivated landscape of the gardening show.

rerseits als wichtiger Beitrag an die Gesamtkultur der Stadt. Die Durchführung eines gemeinsamen Bauforums zur Erstellung eines gemeinschaftlich entwickelten Stadtkonzeptes im Sinne einer Public-Private-Partnership löste Projektideen und Planungsvisionen aus, die nicht allein auf die synergetischen Wechselbeziehungen von Industriebetrieb und Stadtentwicklung ausgerichtet waren, sondern Impulse auch für das Beziehungsgeflecht zwischen Stadt und Landschaft miteinbezogen.

Während Frank O. Gehry den Wiedereinbezug des Rheins in den Stadtorganismus einforderte, bestachen die Entwürfe von Zaha M. Hadid durch die Überhöhung der typischen Landschaftsstrukturen in die angrenzenden Baustrukturen der Stadt. Mit dem Aufgreifen der fast korridorförmigen Landschaftsstrukturen in die Bebauungsgebiete wurde im Falle des Vitra-Komplexes diese selbst zur künstlichen Landschaft.

In dem Workshop von Stadt und Vitra wurde indes aber auch noch eine weitere Perspektive von Alessandro Mendini eröffnet: «Eine Stadt ist nicht nur als Materialisation des Geplanten anzusehen, sondern sie ist darüber hinaus auch Materialisation des Atmosphärischen.» Er schlägt Wege durch die Stadt vor, die dem Einzelnen auch das Sinnliche, das Poetische eröffnen. Der Grundgedanke einer wie auch immer gearteten Verknüpfung von erlebbaren Stationen war hiermit geschaffen – und damit die Verknüpfung zwischen der neuen Stadtkultur um Vitra und der Kulturlandschaft im Zuge der Gartenschau.

Vitra site study
Vitra Standortstudie

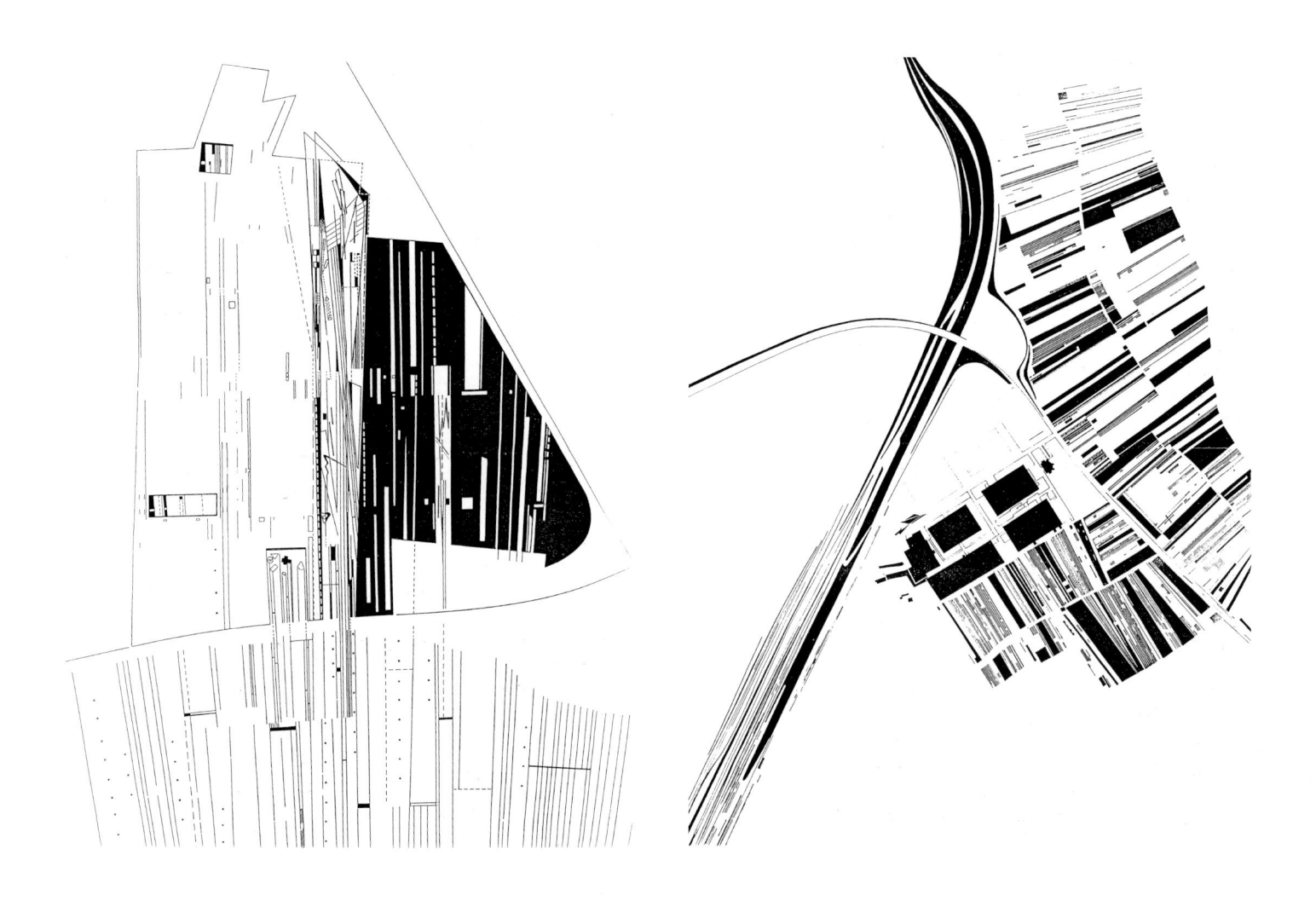

III. The Networking of Vitra Projects with "Grün 99"

In 1992 the characteristics of the location typical for Weil were worked out for the park and gardening show 1999 in a separate building forum of the city of Weil am Rhein on the theme "City-Nature – Urban Nature". In a workshop with well-known landscape architects and urban planners as well as representatives of the city, the new park was seen as the counterpart to the architecturally artistic Vitra complex in the north of the city under the motto "art follows gravel quarrying".

A tangible connection between the spectacular Vitra buildings and a landscaped, architecturally renewed area would be created for the visitor through a route with different stations in the city dealing with special urban task fields. This route concept formed the basis for the competition invitation for the gardening show; its result contained useful suggestions by the landscape architects Krupp, Losert + Partners from Denzlingen which would influence the urban development for the years, if not decades, to come.

Due to financial as well as time-related considerations, the route project from the northern city entrance to the park with the Vitra architecture could not be realized in the short amount of time that remained. Only the redesigns in the inner city, with the conversion of

III. Die Vernetzung von Vitra-Projekten mit der «Grün 99»

Im Jahr 1992 wurden in einem weiteren Bauforum der Stadt Weil am Rhein zur Thematik «Stadt-Natur – Stadtnatur» die Weil-typischen Standortmerkmale für den Park und die Gartenschau im Jahr 1999 erarbeitet. In einem Workshop mit bekannten Landschaftsarchitekten und Städteplanern sowie auch Vertretern der Stadt wurde unter dem Motto «Kunst folgt Kiesabbau» von Dieter Kienast der neue Park als Pendant zum architektonisch kunstvollen Vitrakomplex im Norden der Stadt gesehen.

Über einen Weg mit unterschiedlichen Stationen im Stadtgebiet zu besonderen städtebaulichen Aufgabenfeldern würde auch für den Besucher ein erlebbarer Zusammenhang zwischen den spektakulären Bauten von Vitra und einem landschaftlich-architektonisch innovativen Gebiet hergestellt. Dieses Wegekonzept bildete die Grundlage für die Auslobung des Wettbewerbes zur Landesgartenschau, dessen Ergebnis durch die Arbeit der Landschaftsarchitekten Krupp, Losert + Partner aus Denzlingen städtebaulich nutzbare Vorschläge enthielt, die die weitere Stadtentwicklung für Jahre, wenn nicht gar Jahrzehnte beeinflussen werden.

Aus zeitlichen wie auch finanziellen Erwägungen war das Wegeprojekt vom Stadteingang Nord mit der Vitra-Architektur zum Parkgelände im kurzen verbleibenden Zeitraum nicht umsetzungsfähig. Lediglich die Umgestaltungen in der Innenstadt mit dem Umbau der Hauptstraße und in der denkmalge-

the main street, and in the landmark garden city Leopoldshöhe, were realized. Additional important phases will follow.

The "networking" had to be created via different paths. First considerations, made with Dr Rolf Fehlbaum from Vitra, led to the idea of having special gardens designed by the Vitra architects. This idea, however, was abandoned because of the transitory nature of garden spaces following a gardening show and because the longevity of the relationship between the city and industry could not be symbolized.

The idea of establishing "Follies" (analogous to Bernard Tschumis' Follies in the Parc de la Villette, Paris) as accessible art objects was also abandoned – Bernard Tschumi understood his Follies in the park as a step towards the liberation of architecture that would bring the built form closer to art. What seemed to be in the foreground was the clarification of the special architecture that had meanwhile been found for the location Weil am Rhein in an institution essential to the gardening show and the city: the state pavilion of Baden-Württemberg, connected with spaces for the trinational environmental center in Weil am Rhein. The pavilion offers the guarantee of lasting recognition of a well-developed cooperation between industry and the city that has since arisen. This is not to be understood as a direct act of economic sponsorship but as an expressive symbol of a city that can be proud of its economy.

schützten Gartenstadt Leopoldshöhe wurden realisiert. Weitere wichtige Etappen werden später folgen.

Die «Vernetzung» mußte auf anderen Wegen hergestellt werden. Erste Überlegungen zusammen mit Dr. Rolf Fehlbaum von Vitra führten zur Idee, besondere Gärten durch die Vitra-Architekten anlegen zu lassen. Dieses Szenario wurde jedoch aufgrund der Vergänglichkeit von Gartenräumen nach einer Gartenschau wieder verworfen, da die Dauerhaftigkeit der Beziehung zwischen Stadt und Industrie nicht symbolisiert werden konnte.

Auch die Überlegungen zur Errichtung von «Follies» (analog Bernard Tschumis Follies im Parc de la Villette, Paris) als begehbare Kunstobjekte – Bernard

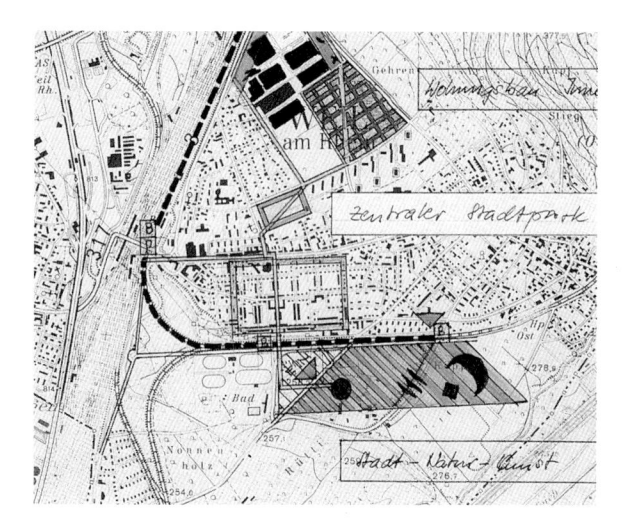

In close cooperation with Dr Rolf Fehlbaum, contact was established with Zaha M. Hadid, who brilliantly mastered a building in a suspenseful dialogue with the genius loci of the landscape in the case of the Vitra fire station appliance building: this was precisely the theme of the planned park in Weil am Rhein.

Klaus Eberhardt
Mayor of the City of Weil am Rhein
Landesgartenschau 1999 GmbH

Tschumi sah seine Follies im Park als ein Schritt zur Befreiung der Architektur, die die gebaute Form näher zur Kunst bringt – wurden wieder fallengelassen. Von primärer Wichtigkeit erschien vielmehr die Verdeutlichung der mittlerweile für den Standort Weil am Rhein gefundenen, besonderen Architektur in einer für die Gartenschau und Stadt notwendigen Einrichtung: dem Landespavillon Baden-Württemberg verbunden mit Räumen für das Trinationale Umweltzentrum in Weil am Rhein. Der gebaute Pavillon allein bietet die Gewähr einer dauerhaften Erkennbarkeit der gut entwickelten Zusammenarbeit zwischen Industrie und Stadt. Kein direkter Akt der Wirtschaftsförderung, aber ausdruckstarkes Zeichen einer Stadt, die stolz auf ihre Wirtschaft sein kann.

In enger Zusammenarbeit mit Dr. Rolf Fehlbaum wurden Kontakte zur Zaha M. Hadid geknüpft, die es beim Feuerwehrgerätehaus Vitra meisterlich verstanden hatte, ein Gebäude in einem spannungsvollen Dialog mit dem Genius loci der Landschaft zu schaffen: eben genau der Themenstellung für den geplanten Park in Weil am Rhein.

Klaus Eberhardt
Bürgermeister Stadt Weil am Rhein
Landesgartenschau 1999 GmbH

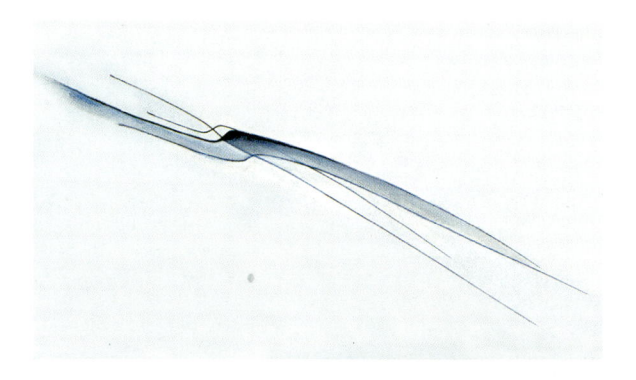

Landscape study
Landschaftsstudie

LF one, Weil am Rhein
Natural and Artificial Landscape Formations

The project is designed to serve as an event and exhibition space for the gardening show in Weil am Rhein 1999. Rather than being articulated as an isolated object, the building is physically and formally embedded in the large and topographically rich garden-scape.

The built spaces emerge gently from the fluid geometry of the surrounding network of paths, three of which entangle to form the building: one path snuggles up to the south side of the building, while another, gently sloping, rises over its back; the third describes a shallow S-curve and cuts diagonally through the interior.

Four parallel and partly interwoven spaces are caught in this bundle of paths. The two main spaces – exhibition hall and café – are stretched along the contours of these paths, allowing for ample light and visibility.

Ancillary rooms disappear within the "root" of the building. An outdoor terrace is located to the south of the café, continuing its slightly sunken floor level. Another part of the programme – a small environmental research centre – is situated north of the exhibition hall, partly shifted into the volume of the hall and submerged into the ground to take advantage of the earth as a climatic buffer. The roof over

LF one, Weil am Rhein
Natürliche und künstliche Landschaftsformationen

Das Projekt soll als Veranstaltungs- und Ausstellungsraum für die Landesgartenschau 1999 in Weil am Rhein dienen. Es ist nicht als isoliertes Objekt artikuliert, sondern physisch und formell in die große, topographisch abwechslungsreiche Gartenlandschaft integriert.

Die gebauten Räume steigen sanft aus der fließenden Geometrie eines sie umgebenden Wegenetzes auf; drei der Wege verzweigen sich und geben dem Gebäude seine Form: Ein Weg schmiegt sich an die Südseite des Baus an, während ein anderer leicht ansteigt und oberhalb der Rückseite endet; der dritte Weg in Form einer flachen S-Kurve, schneidet sich diagonal durch das Innere des Gebäudes hindurch.

In diesem Wegebündel sind vier parallele und teilweise miteinander verbundene Räume entstanden. Die beiden Haupträume – Ausstellungshalle und Café – erstrecken sich entlang den Konturen dieser Wege und erlauben einen großzügigen Lichteinfall ins Innere sowie einen guten Ausblick nach draußen.

Die Nebenräume verschwinden in der «Wurzel» des Gebäudes. Eine Terrasse samt Veranstaltungsraum setzt südlich des Cafés die leicht abgesenkte Geschoßebene fort. Ein weiterer Teil des Bauprogramms – ein kleines Umweltforschungszentrum – befindet sich nördlich der Ausstellungshalle, ist teilweise in deren Volumen integriert und in den Boden

the sunken centre becomes an open mezzanine within the exhibition space. This mezzanine in turn participates in a second route through the building linking the raised public path to the path intersecting the building, at ground level.

The space-bundle "LF one" for the gardening show (Landesgartenschau 1999, Weil am Rhein) is part of a sequence of projects that try to elicit new fluid spatialities from the study of natural landscape formations such as river deltas, mountain ranges, forests, deserts, canyons, ice-flows, oceans and so on.

The most important general characteristics we look for in landscape spaces, in distinction to traditional urban and architectural spaces, are the multitude and subtleties of territorial definitions as well as the smoothness of transitions between spaces. Both characteristics, which from a traditional architectural vantage point might be regarded as lacking in order and definition, allow more complex and nuanced order of spaces and activities. Realms interpenetrate; distinctions are vague and latent rather than definitive and frozen. These latent distinctions and spatial definitions are revealed and amplified by the temporary activities that hook on to features that might otherwise remain mute and unobtrusive. Landscape spaces remain flexible and open, not due to a modernist blank neutrality, but by virtue of an overabundance and simultaneity of soft articulations. Whereas architecture generally channels, seg-

vertieft, um die klimatische Pufferwirkung der Erde zu nutzen. Das Dach über dem abgesenkten Zentrum wird im Ausstellungsraum zum offenen Zwischengeschoß. Dieses wiederum ist an einen zweiten Weg durch das Gebäude angeschlossen und verbindet den erhöhten öffentlichen Weg mit dem Weg, der das Gebäude auf der Erdgeschoßebene durchdringt.

Das Raumbündel «LF one» für die Landesgartenschau 1999 in Weil am Rhein ist Teil einer Projektreihe, die versucht, neue und fließende Räumlichkeiten aus dem Studium der natürlichen Landschaftsformationen – z. B. Flußdeltas, Gebirge, Wälder, Wüsten, Schluchten, Eisschollen, Ozeane – abzuleiten.

Die wichtigsten Eigenschaften, die wir in Landschaftsräumen suchen – im Unterschied zu den traditionellen städtischen und architektonischen Räumen –, sind Vielfältigkeit und Feinheiten der territorialen Definitionen sowie die Weichheit der Übergänge zwischen diesen Räumen. Beide Eigenschaften, denen aus traditioneller architektonischer Perspektive ein Mangel an Ordnung und Definition nachgesagt werden könnte, ermöglichen uns eine komplexere und nuancenreichere Anordnung der Räume und Aktivitäten. Verschiedene Bereiche überschneiden sich, Unterschiede sind nur vage angedeutet, statt definitiv und erstarrt zu sein. Latente Unterschiede und räumliche Definitionen werden durch vorübergehende Aktivitäten, die sich an die Eigenschaften anknüpfen, die ansonsten still und unaufdringlich bleiben würden, offenbart und betont. Landschaftsräume bleiben flexibel und offen, und dies nicht auf-

Study model
Arbeitsmodell

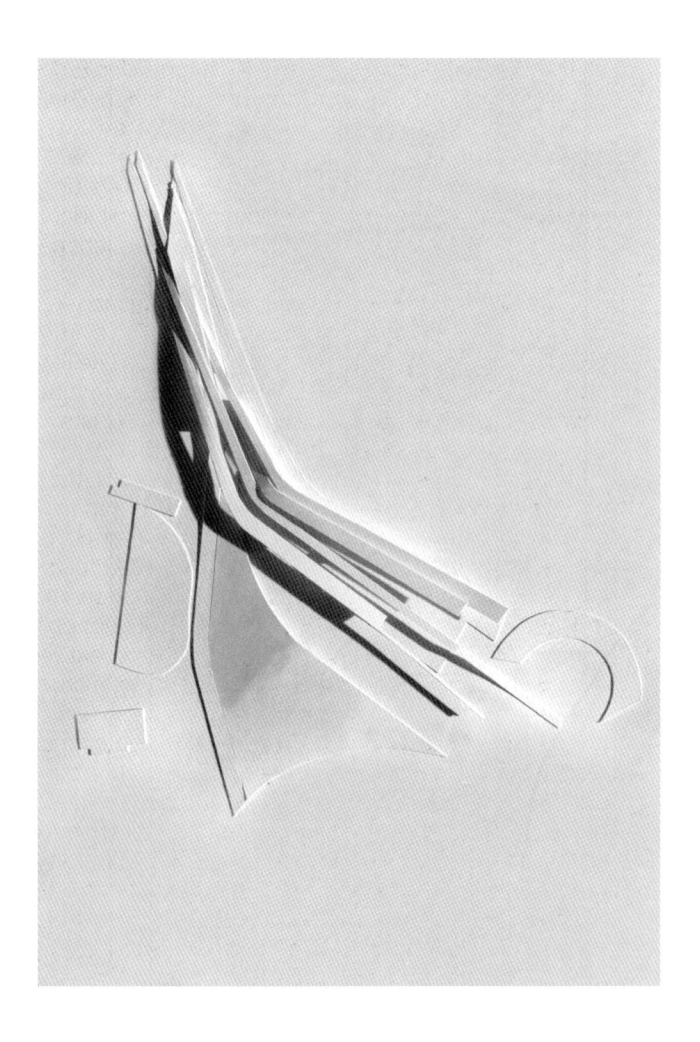

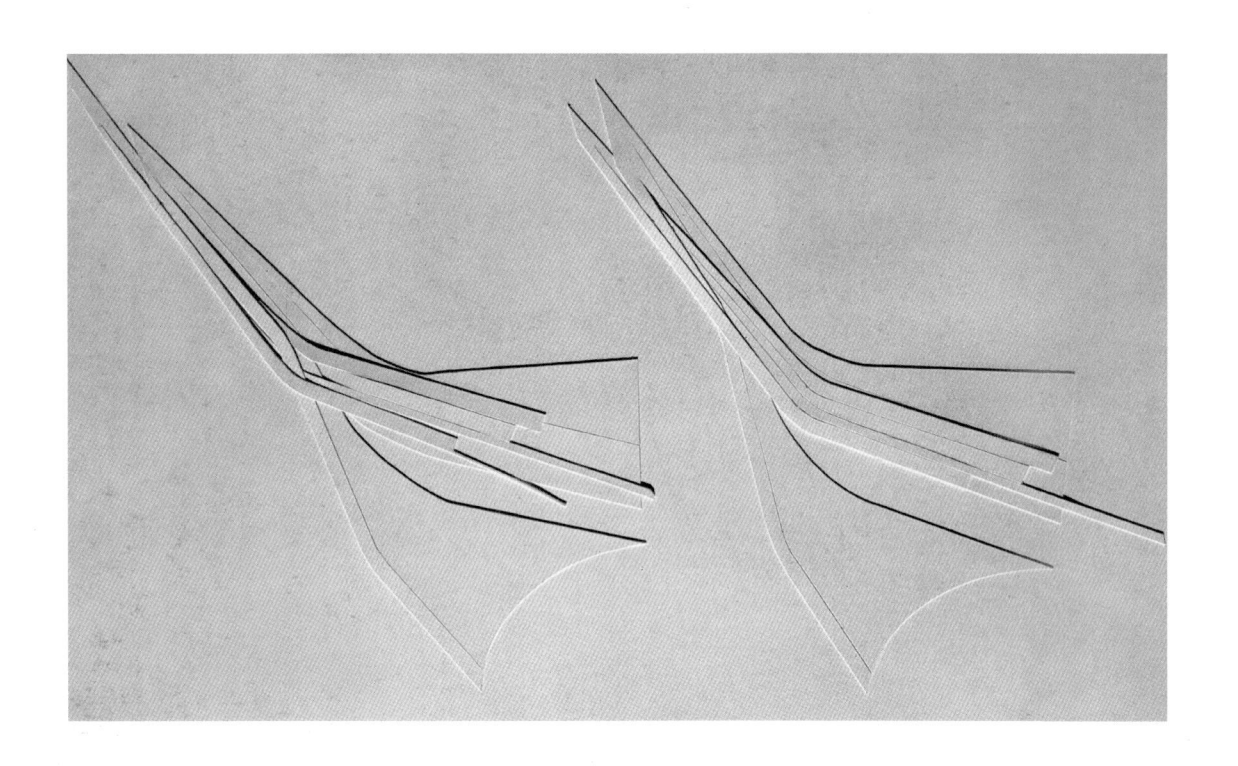

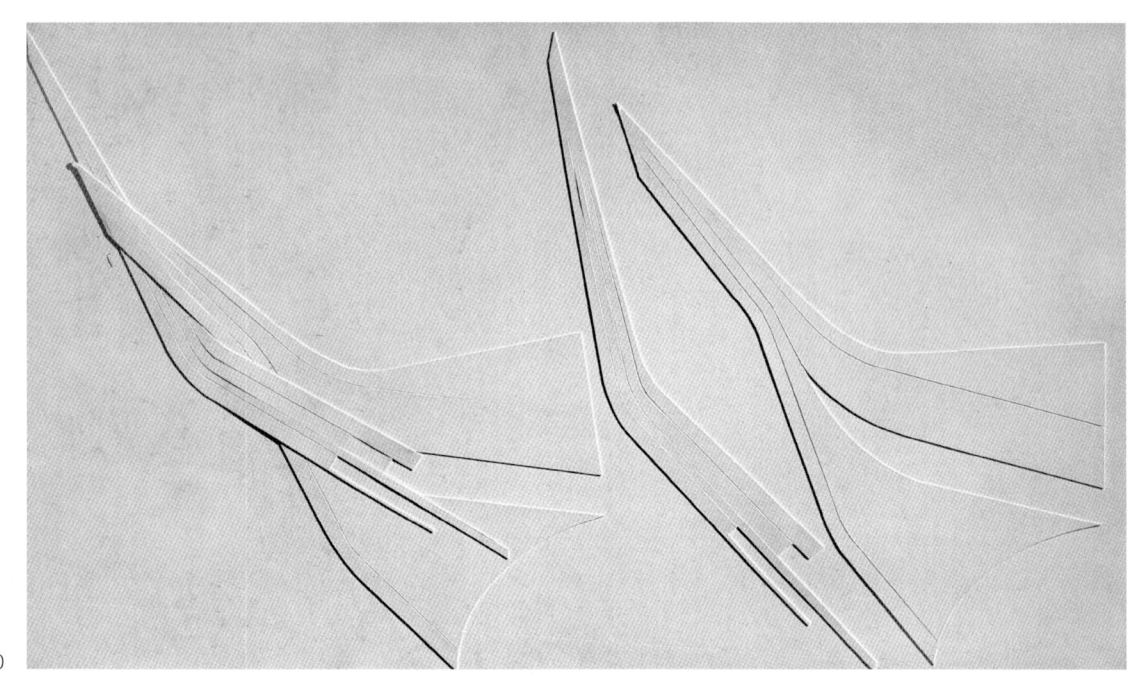

Ground study
Topographisches
Modell

ments and closes, landscape opens, offers and suggests.

This does not mean that we abandon architecture and surrender to brute nature. The point here is to seek out potentially productive analogies to inspire the invention of new artificial scapes and landforms, pertinent to our contemporary complex, multiple and transient life processes.

grund einer modernen, schlichten Neutralität, sondern durch den Überfluß und die Gleichzeitigkeit sanfter Artikulationen. Im Gegensatz zur Architektur, die im allgemeinen kanalisiert, segmentiert und verschließt, öffnet die Landschaft, sie unterbreitet Angebote und Vorschläge.

Das bedeutet nicht, daß wir die Architektur aufgeben und uns der rauhen Natur unterwerfen wollen. Hier geht es darum, potentiell produktive Analogien ausfindig zu machen, die zur Erfindung neuer, künstlicher Räume und Landformen inspirieren, welche für unsere komplexen, vielfältigen und vergänglichen modernen Lebensprozesse relevant sind.

Site study
Geländestudie

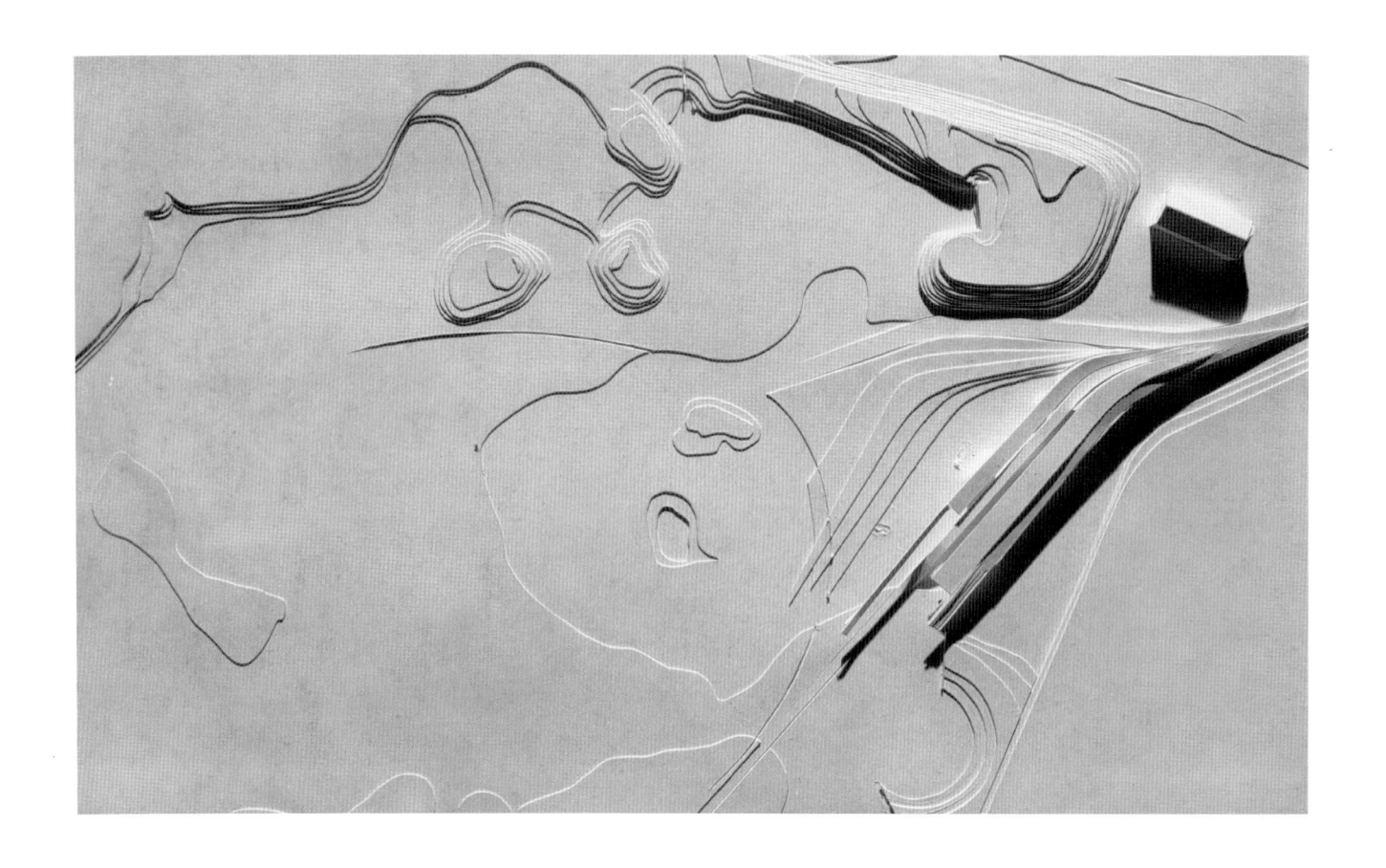

Landscape study
Topographischer Lageplan

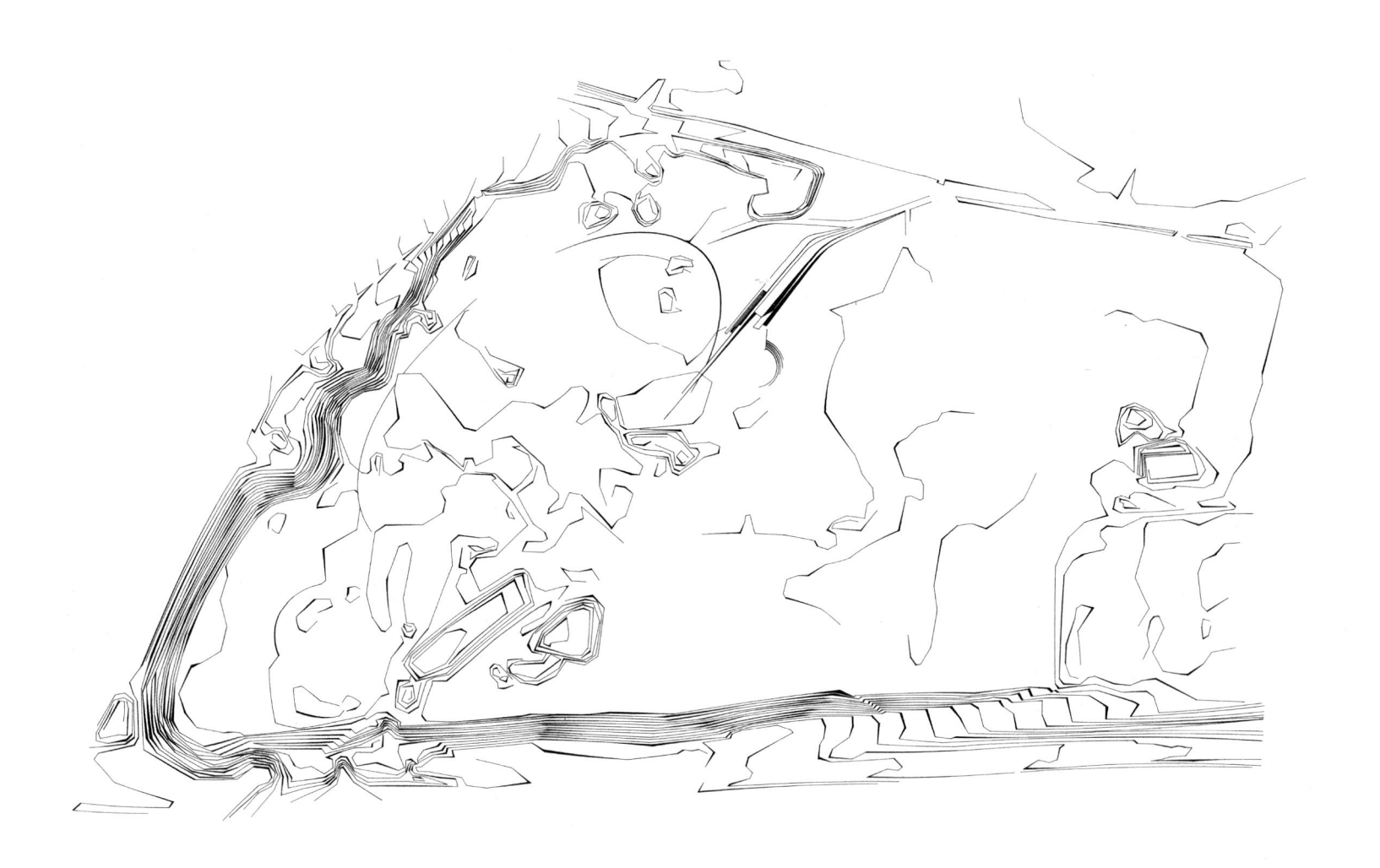

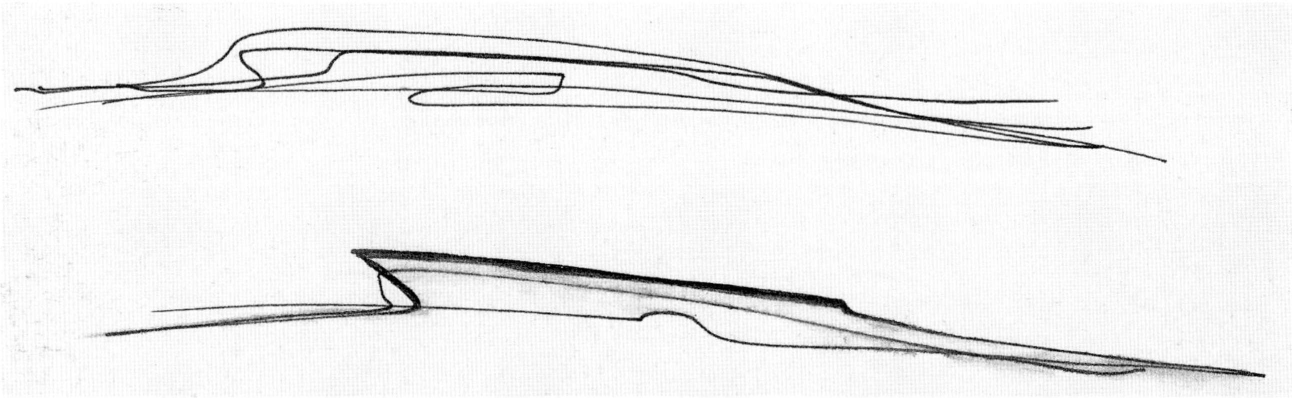

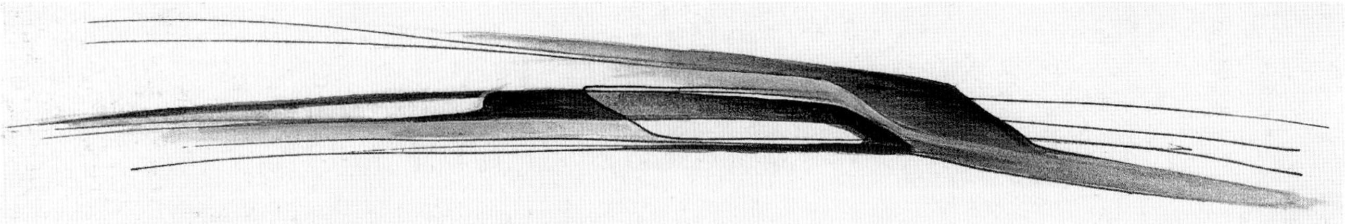

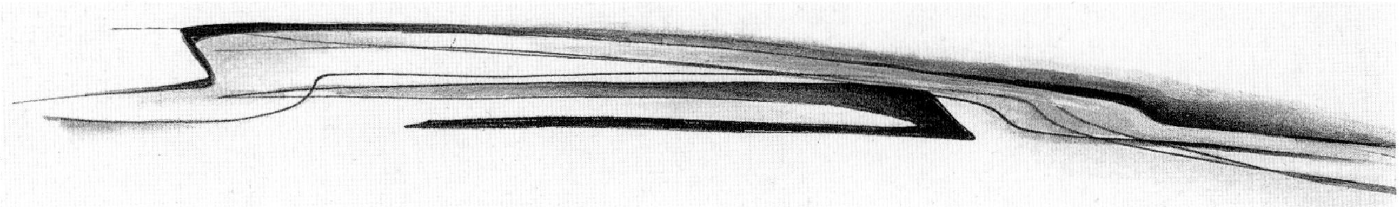

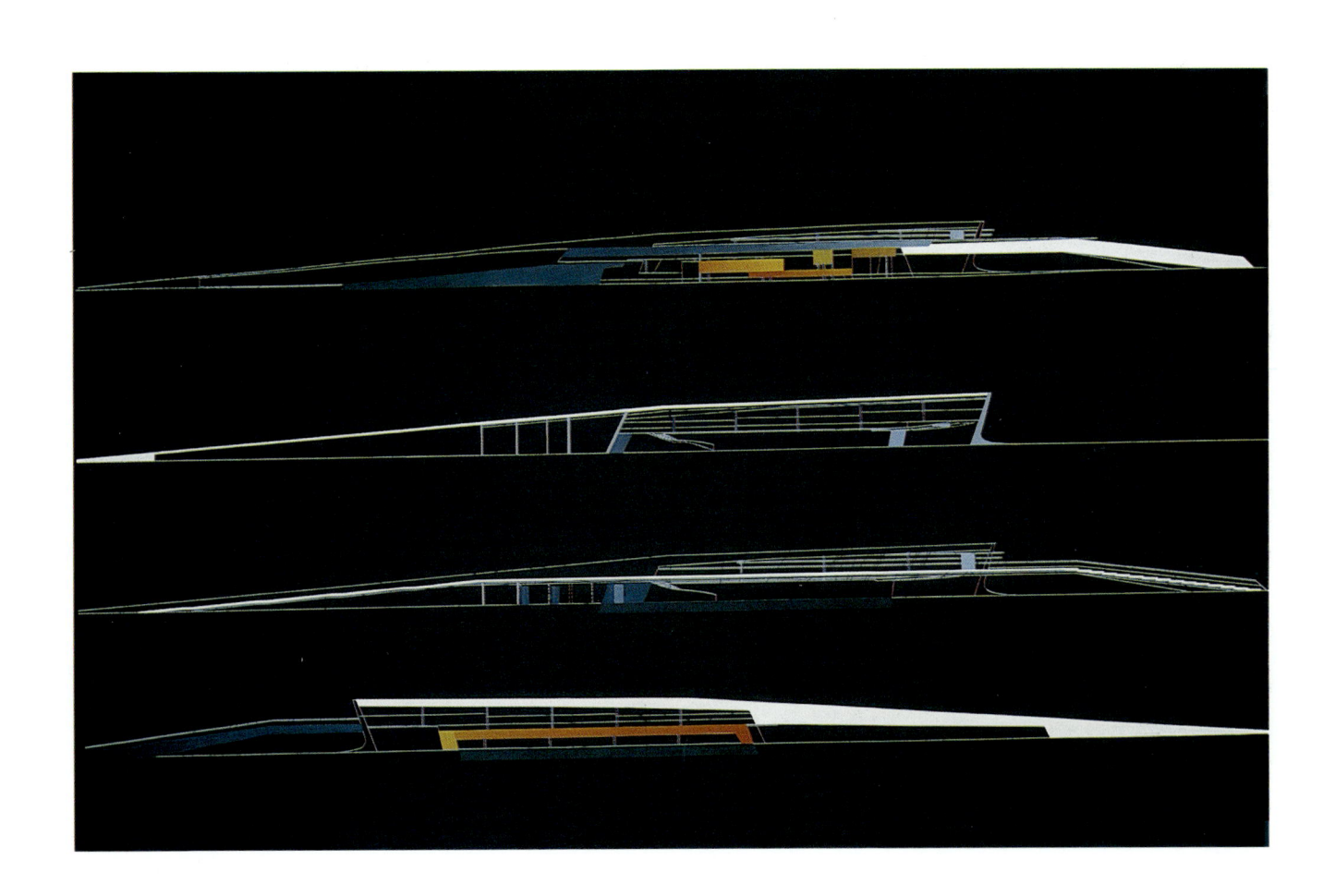

Elevation/section, painting
Ansicht/Schnitte, Painting

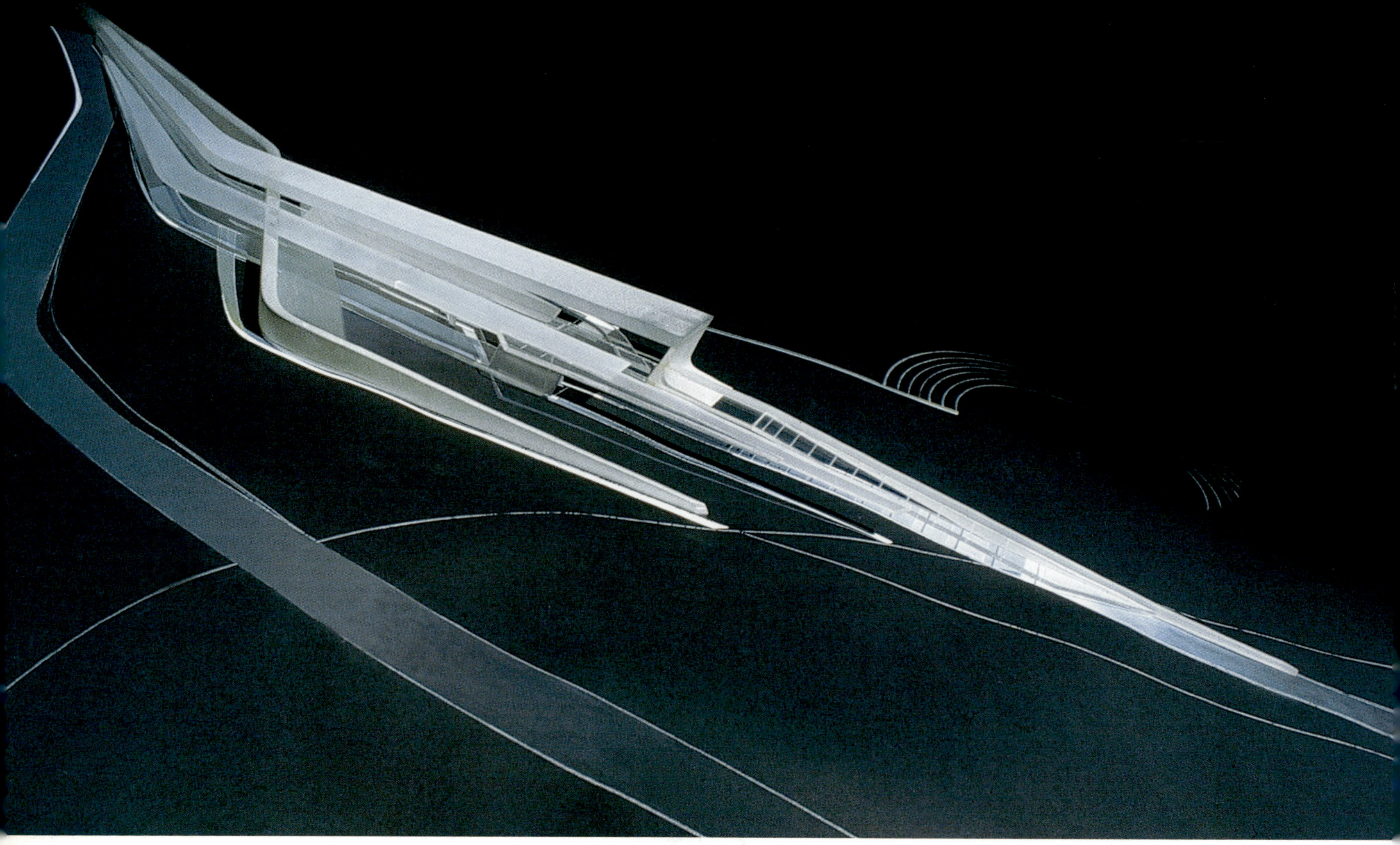

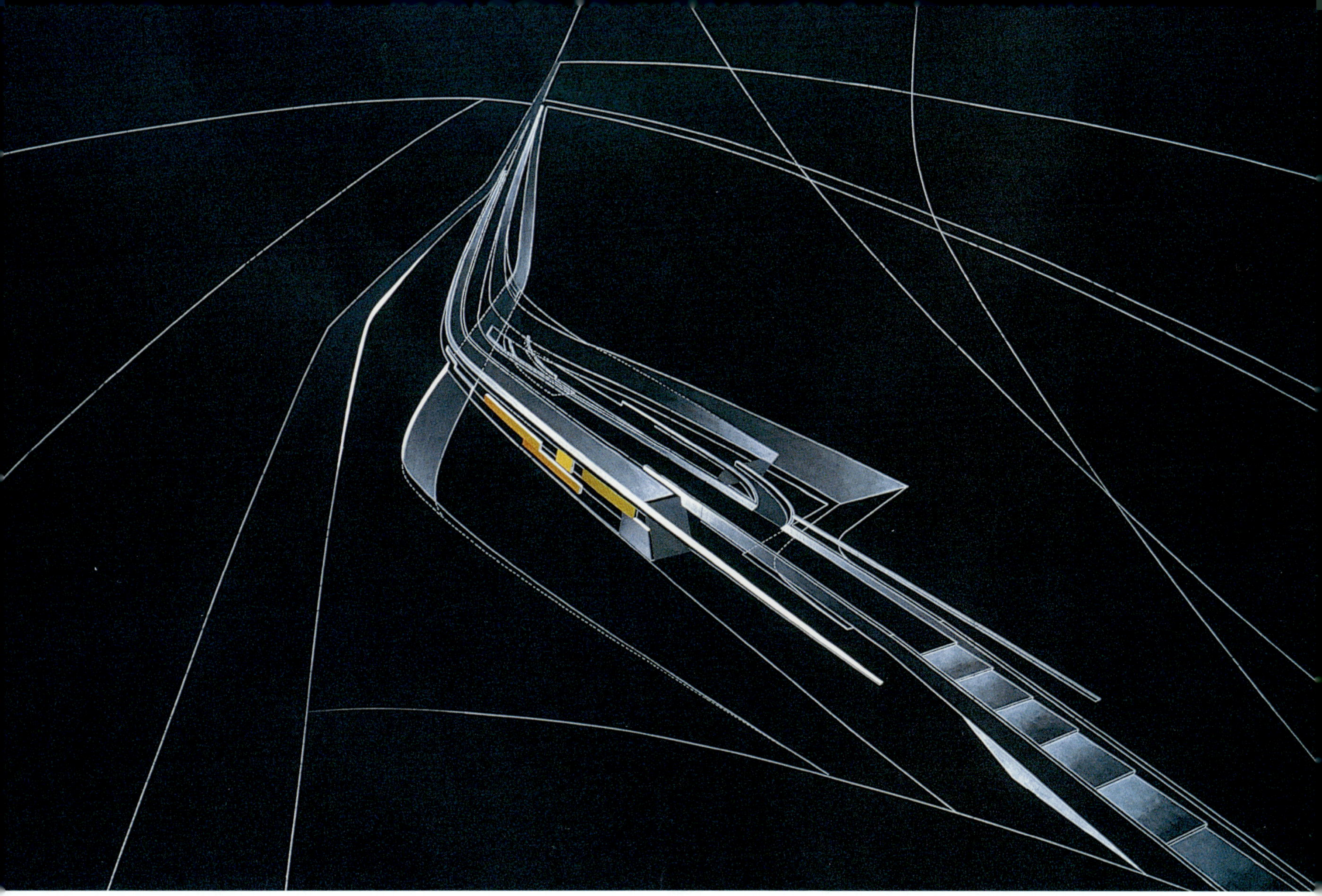

The space-bundle realizes some of the aspects of landscape that we have identified as most liberating: the figure of our building is not contained. It literally bleeds out and dissolves into the surrounding landscape. It emerges gradually from the tangle of paths, leaving it to the visitor to define and realize its beginning and end, according to his or her perspective, purpose or mood.

Also, the size and boundary of the building is rendered soft as its order and geometry ripples out into the garden scape, via the sunken terrace and the adjacent southern path, which is articulated as one more contour in the sequence of related lines, cascading down from the highest roof edge.

The rigid distinction between circulation space and occupied space is blurred via an overabundance of potential movement spaces and the overall fluid geometry.

The ground plane as stable reference is subverted through its multiplication. The public path sweeping over the building and the terrace carving into the ground makes any definition of "ground" ambiguous.

The levels within and around the building are subtly staggered, so that they may potentially congregate into a single event, while allowing for temporary (or simultaneous) intimacy.

Multiple competing fluid boundaries abound in the interior and blur the interior-exterior dichotomy: column rows are misaligned

Das Raumbündel setzt einige der landschaftlichen Aspekte um, die wir als die befreiendsten erkannt haben: Die Form des Gebäudes ist nicht beherrscht. Es blutet buchstäblich aus und verschmilzt mit der umliegenden Landschaft. Es erhebt sich allmählich aus dem Wegenetz, wobei es den Besuchern überlassen bleibt – je nach deren Perspektive, Ziel oder Stimmung – seinen Anfang und sein Ende zu definieren und zu erkennen.

Größe und Grenzen des Gebäudes sind weich gestaltet, während seine Ordnung und Geometrie über die abgesenkte Terrasse und den angrenzenden südlichen Weg in die Gartenlandschaft hinausplätschern; der Weg ist in der Abfolge der sich aufeinander beziehenden Linien als zusätzliche Kontur artikuliert und fällt von der höchsten Dachkante nach unten ab.

Die strenge Unterscheidung zwischen dem Erschließungsraum und dem benutzten Raum wird durch eine Überfülle an potentiellen Bewegungsräumen und die insgesamt fließende Geometrie verwischt. Der Grundriß als stabiler Bezugspunkt wurde durch seine Multiplikation aufgehoben. Der öffentliche Weg, der sich über das Gebäude hinzieht, und die Terrasse, die sich in den Grund einschneidet, verleihen der Definition von «Grund» Mehrdeutigkeit.

Die Ebenen im Gebäude und außerhalb davon sind leicht abgestuft, so daß sie potentiell für einen bestimmten Anlaß zusammengeführt werden können, während sie ebenso die zeitweilige (oder gleichzeitige) Intimität ermöglichen.

Mehrere konkurrierende, fließende Grenzen bündeln sich im Inneren und verwischen die Dichotomie

through level shifts in the floor which are countered by shifts in the ceiling, continuous geometries cut against the facade and thermal definition of the interior. The result is a compressed space full of overlap and visual oscillation, as alignments, rhythms and textures are played off against each other.

Office Zaha Hadid

von Innen und Außen: Stützpfeilerreihen wurden durch die unterschiedlichen Ebenen des Fußbodens aus der Reihe gebracht; diese werden wiederum von Verschiebungen in der Decke gekontert; fortlaufende Geometrien enden in der Fassade und an der thermischen Definition des Innenraumes. Das Ergebnis ist ein komprimierter Raum, voll von Überschneidungen und visuellen Oszillationen, in dem gleichzeitig Aufreihungen, Rhythmen und Texturen gegeneinander ausgespielt werden.

Office Zaha Hadid

Study model
Arbeitsmodell

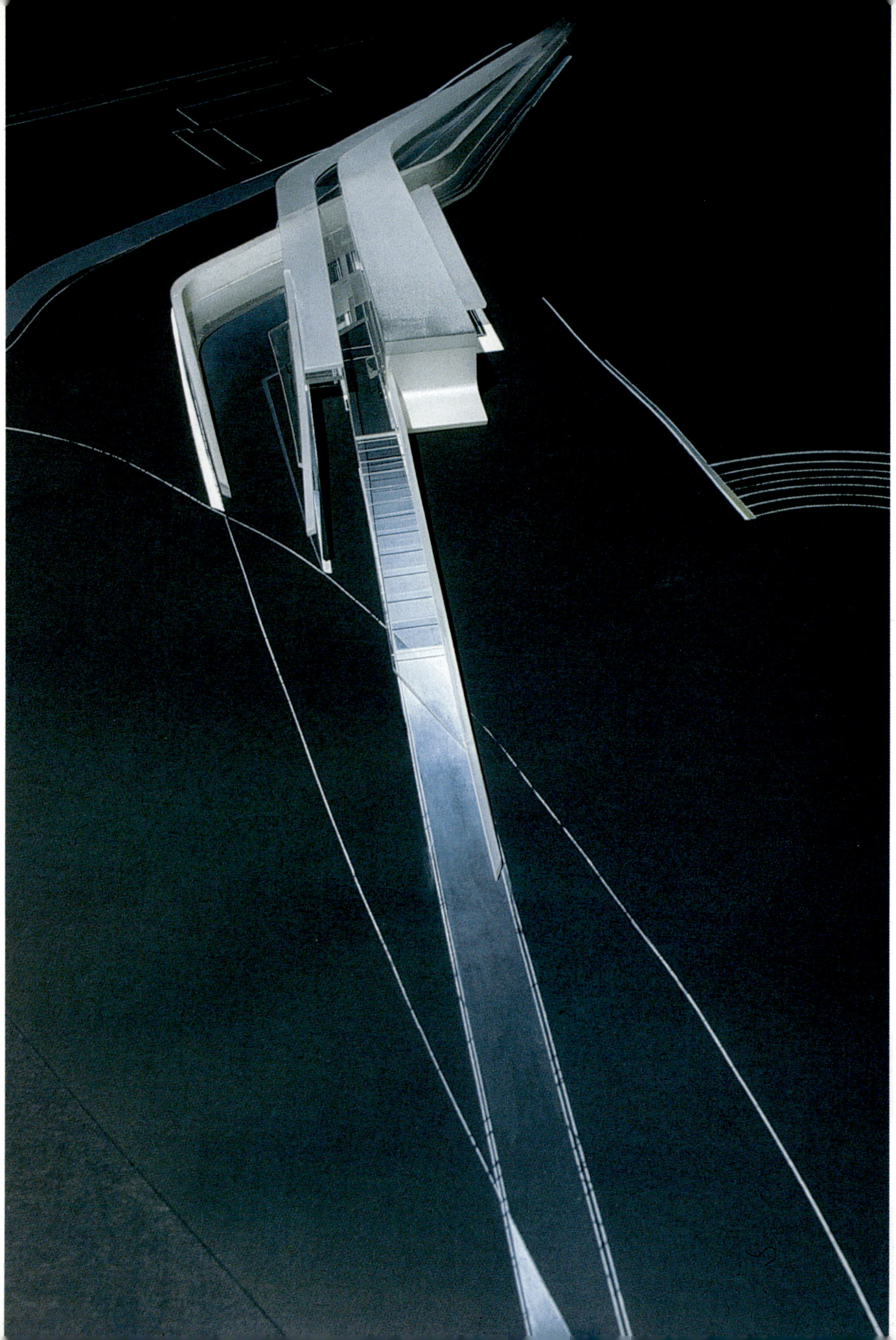

"Vase"

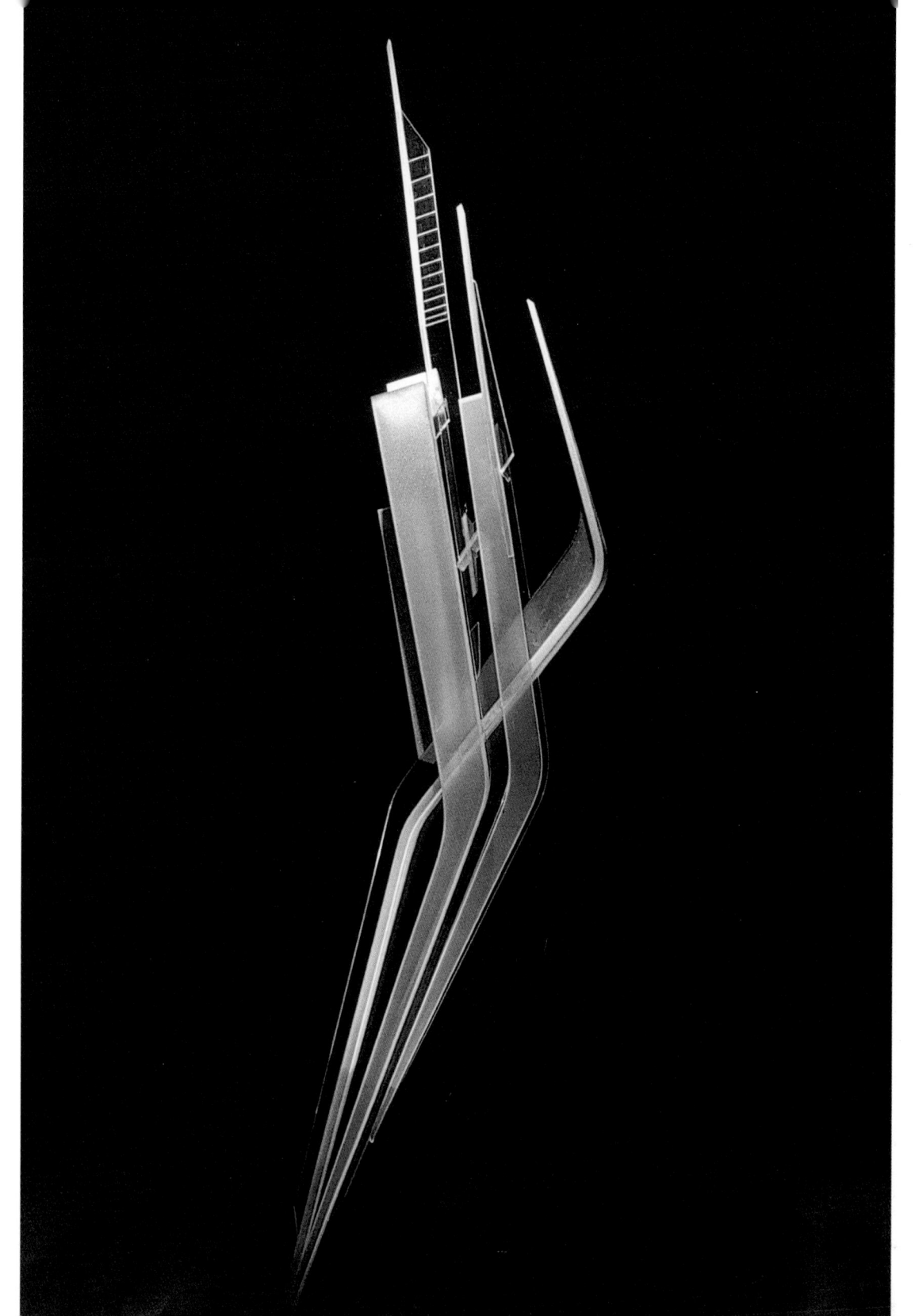

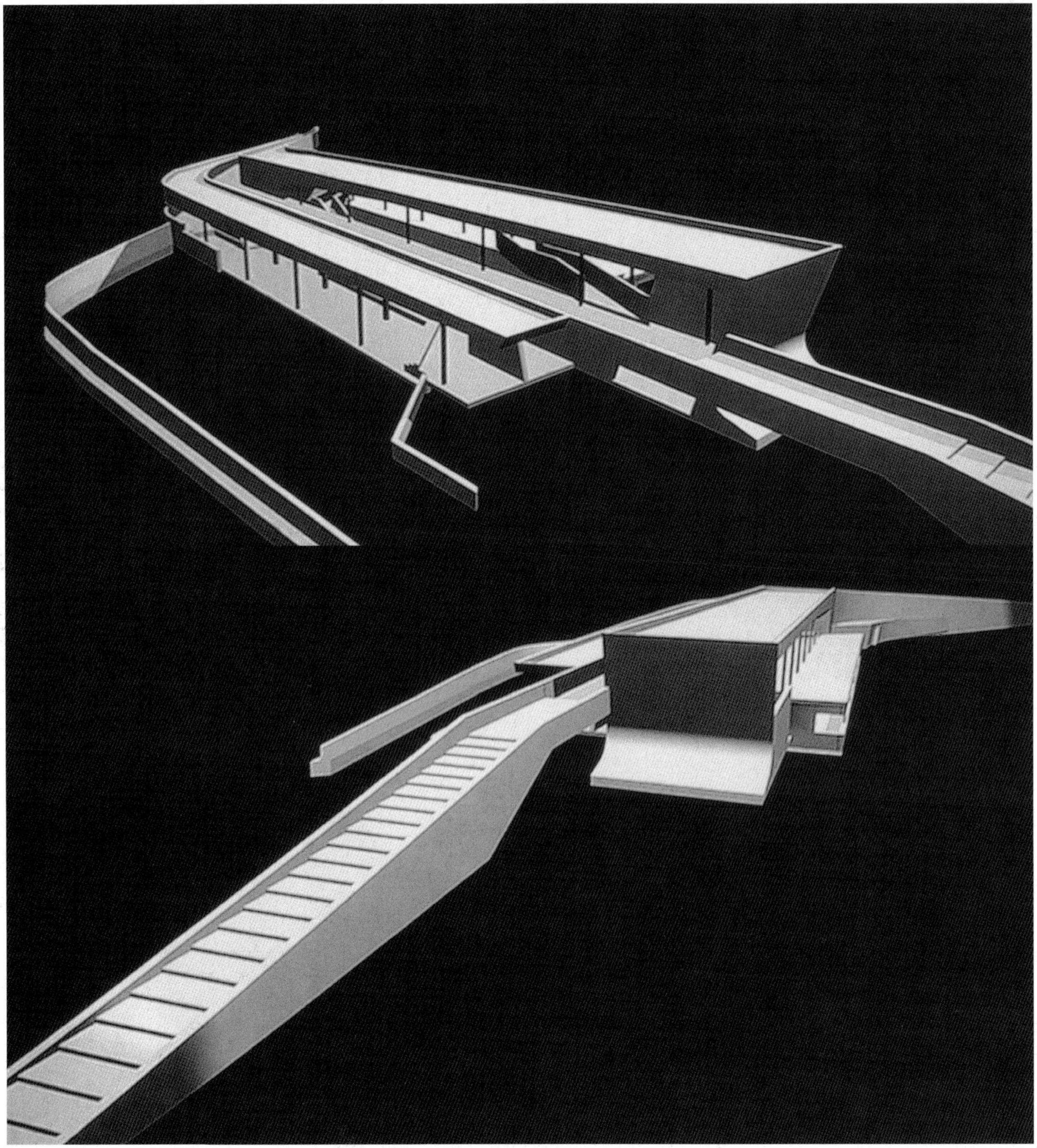

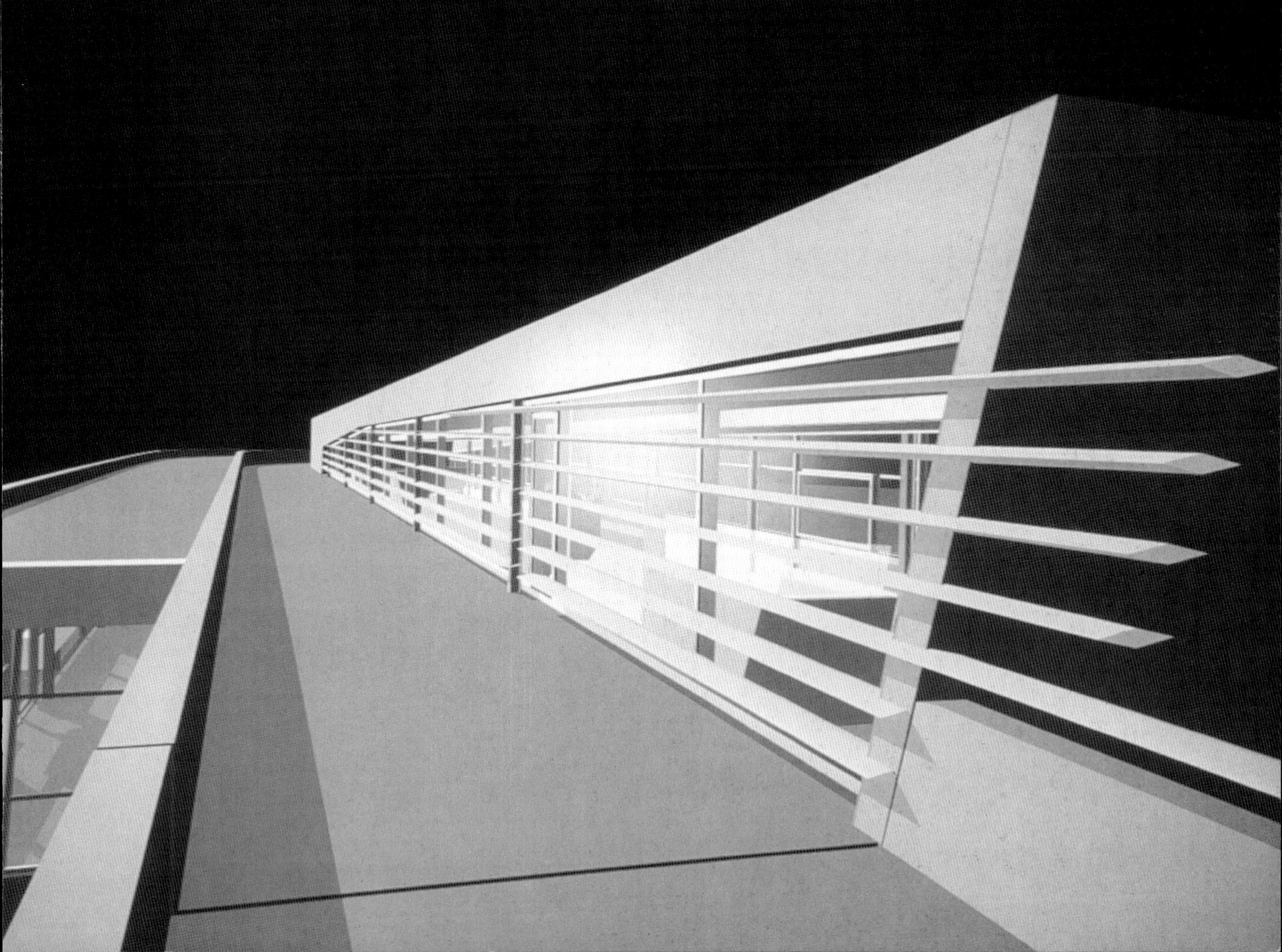

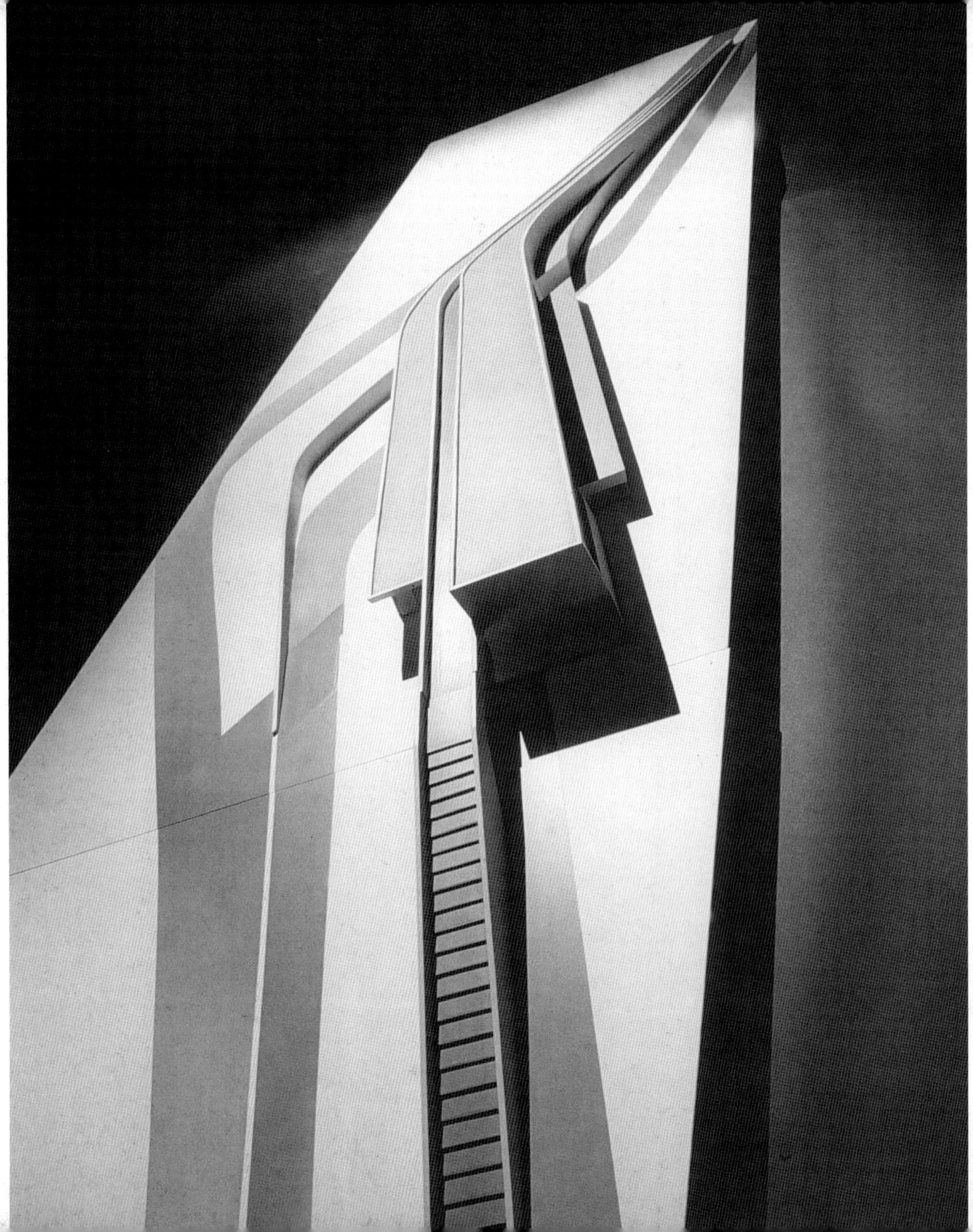

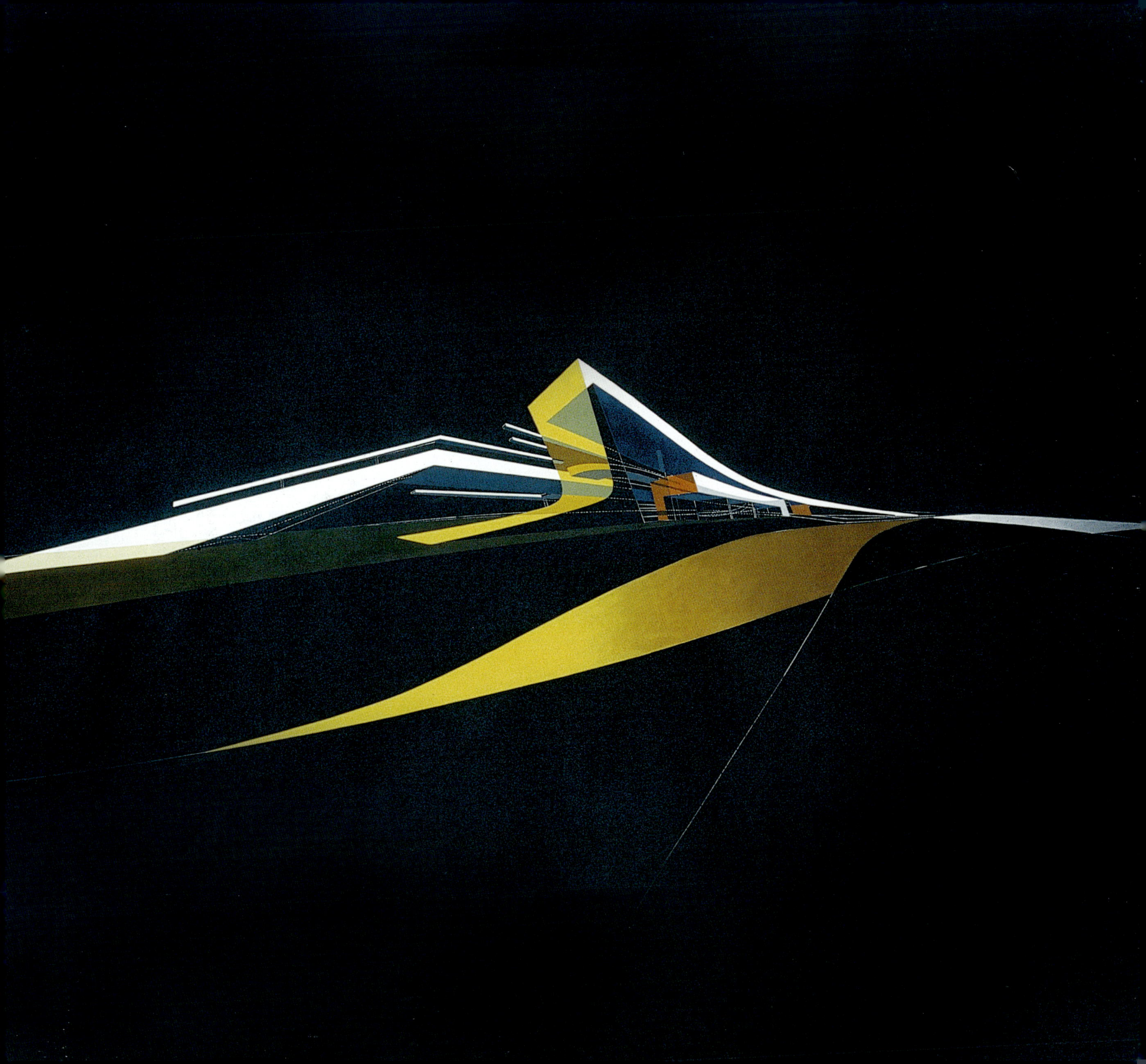

36

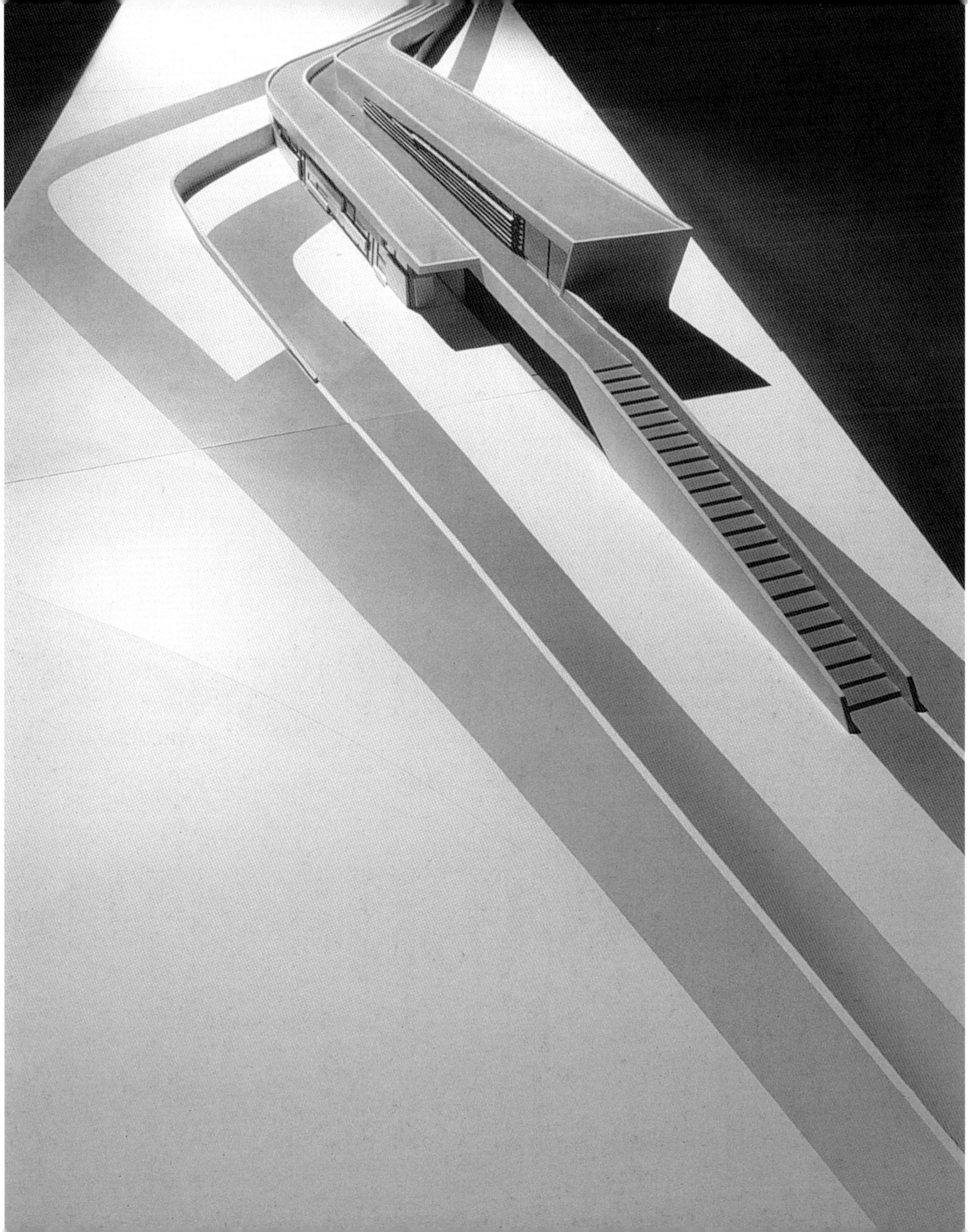

38

39

Plan, section study
Plan/Schnittstudie

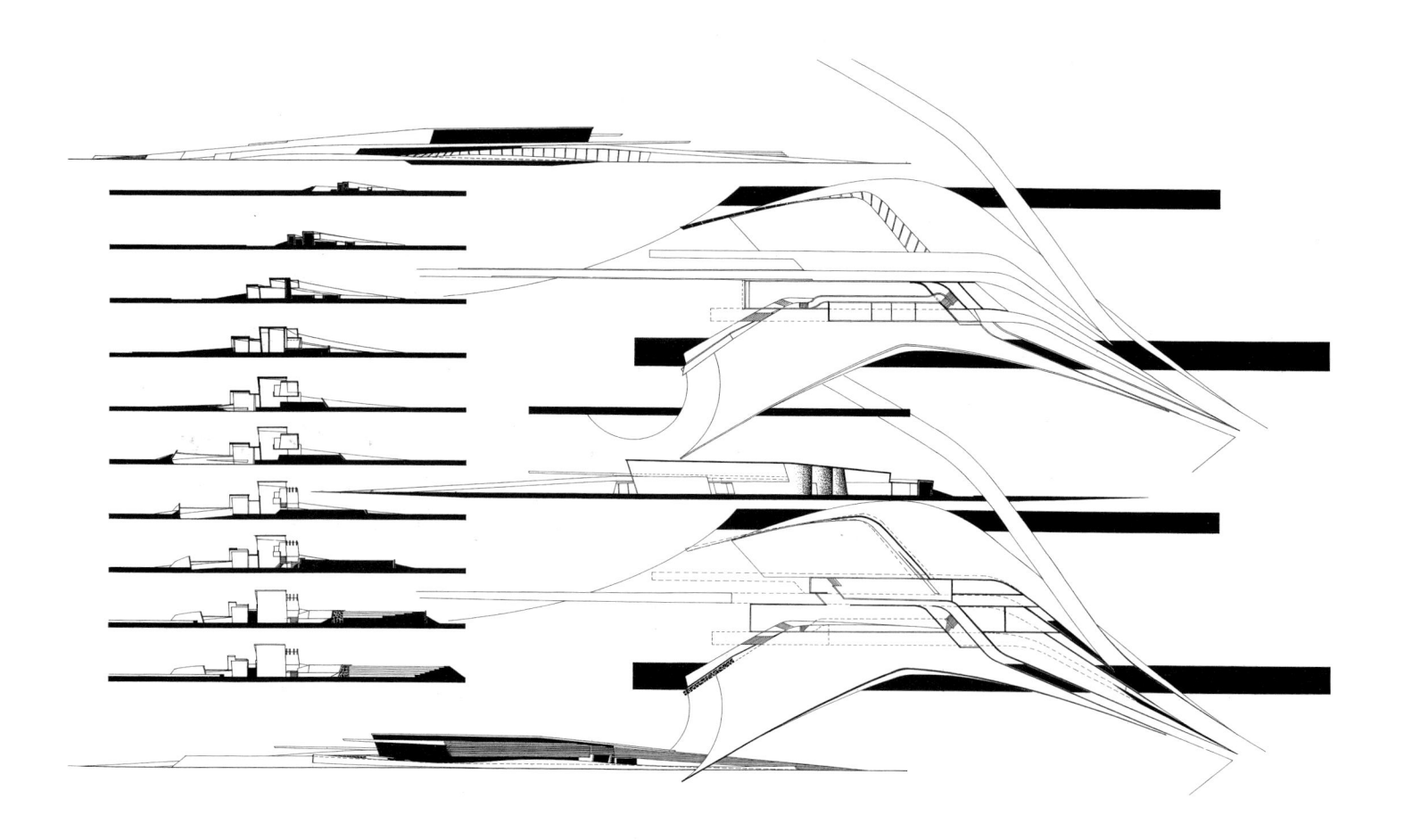

Site plan
Lageplan

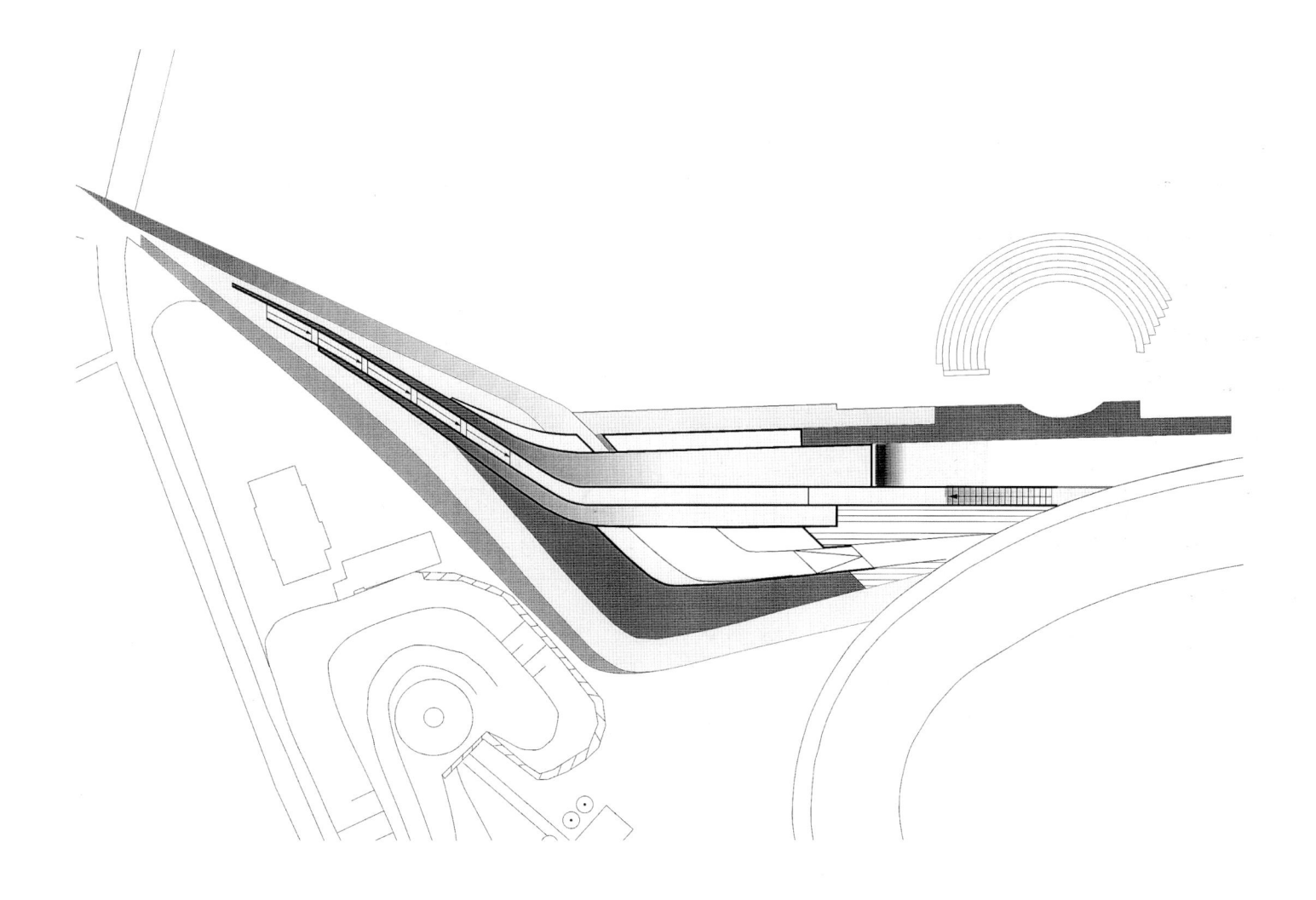

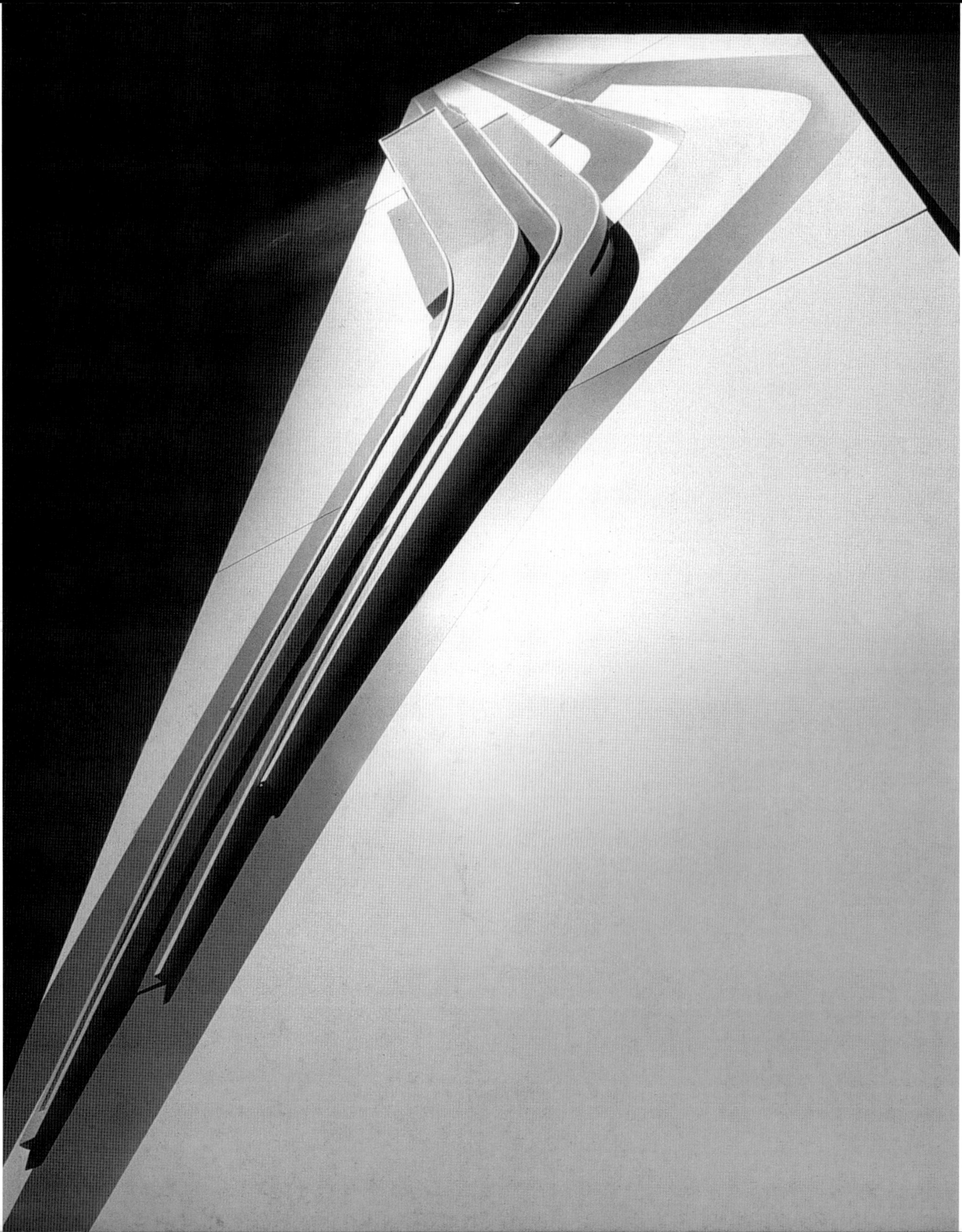

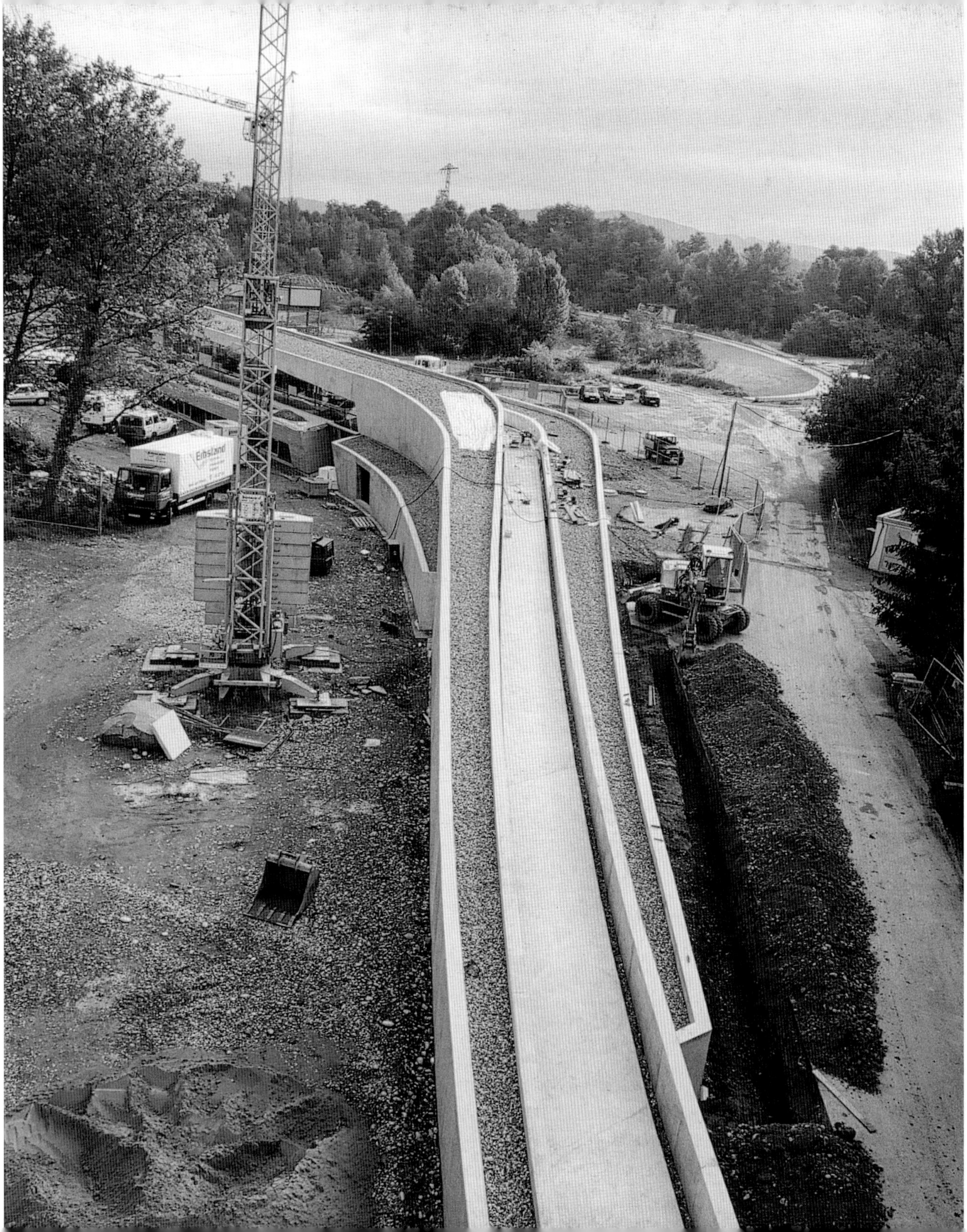

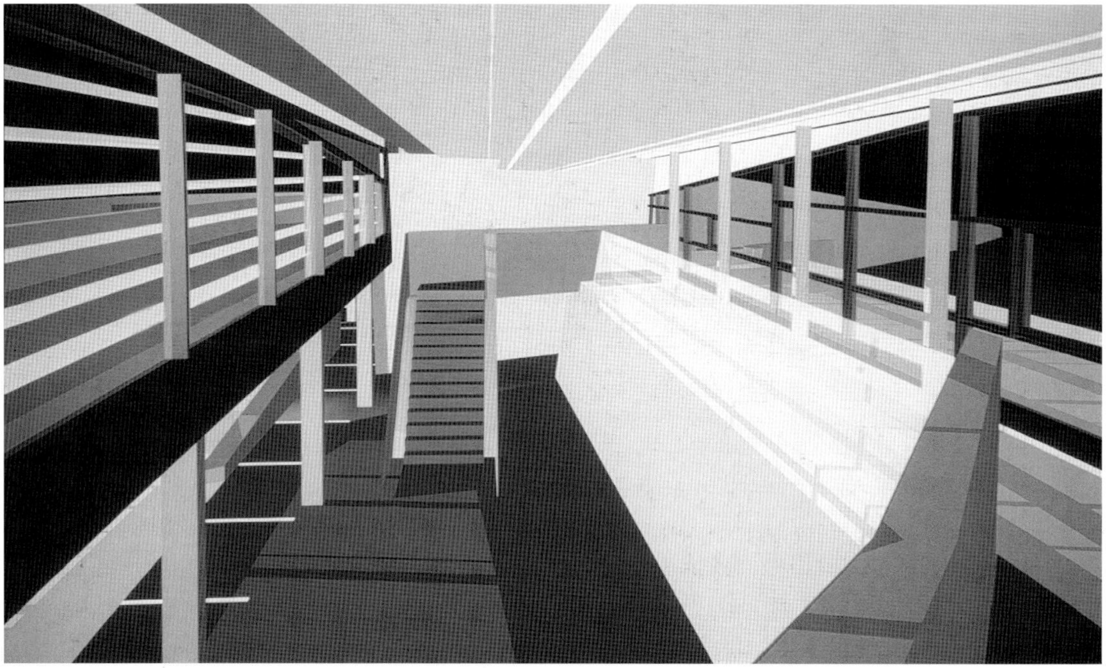

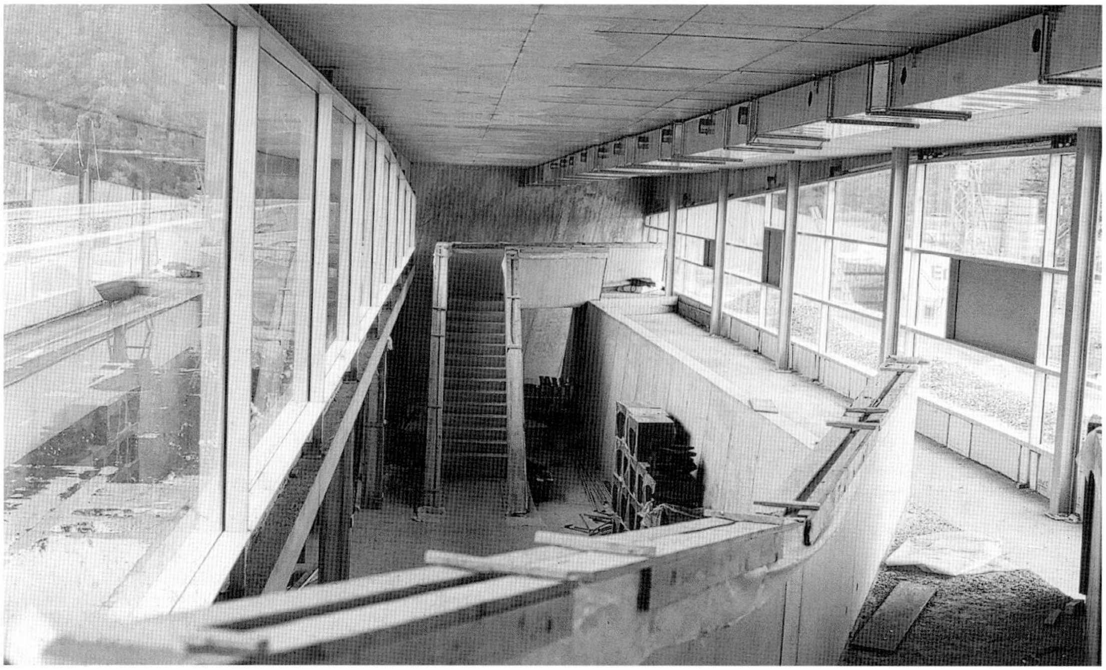

45

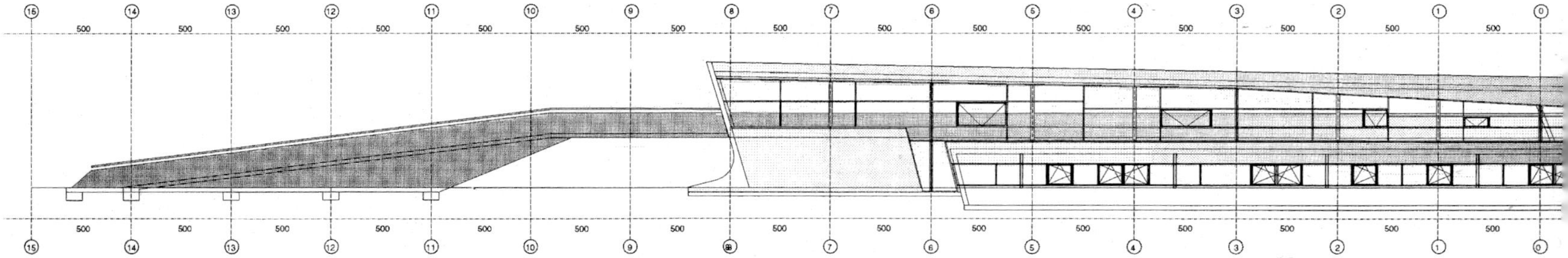
15 14 13 12 11 10 9 8 7 6 5 4 3 2 1 0
500 500 500 500 500 500 500 500 500 500 500 500 500 500 500
500 500 500 500 500 500 500 500 500 500 500 500 500 500 500
15 14 13 12 11 10 9 8 7 6 5 4 3 2 1 0

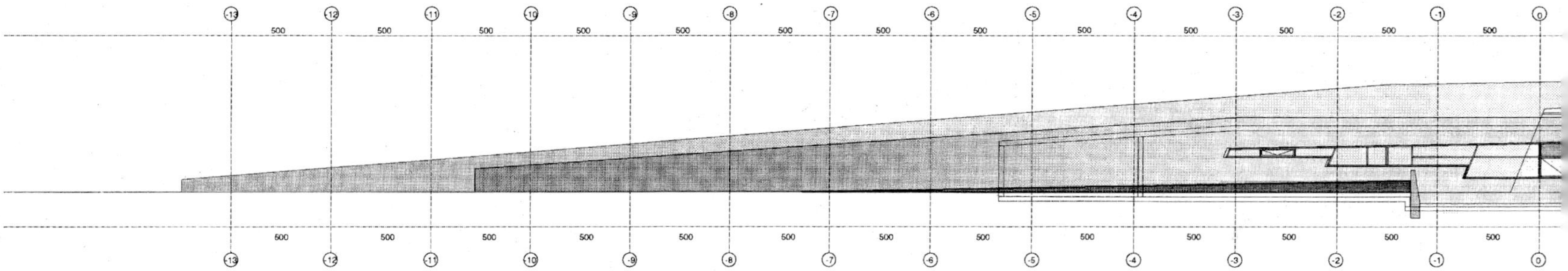
-13 -12 -11 -10 -9 -8 -7 -6 -5 -4 -3 -2 -1 0
500 500 500 500 500 500 500 500 500 500 500 500 500
500 500 500 500 500 500 500 500 500 500 500 500 500
-13 -12 -11 -10 -9 -8 -7 -6 -5 -4 -3 -2 -1 0

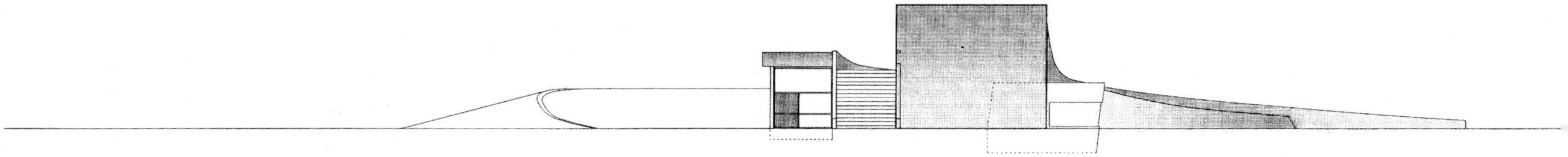

North-West elevation
Ansicht, Nordwesten

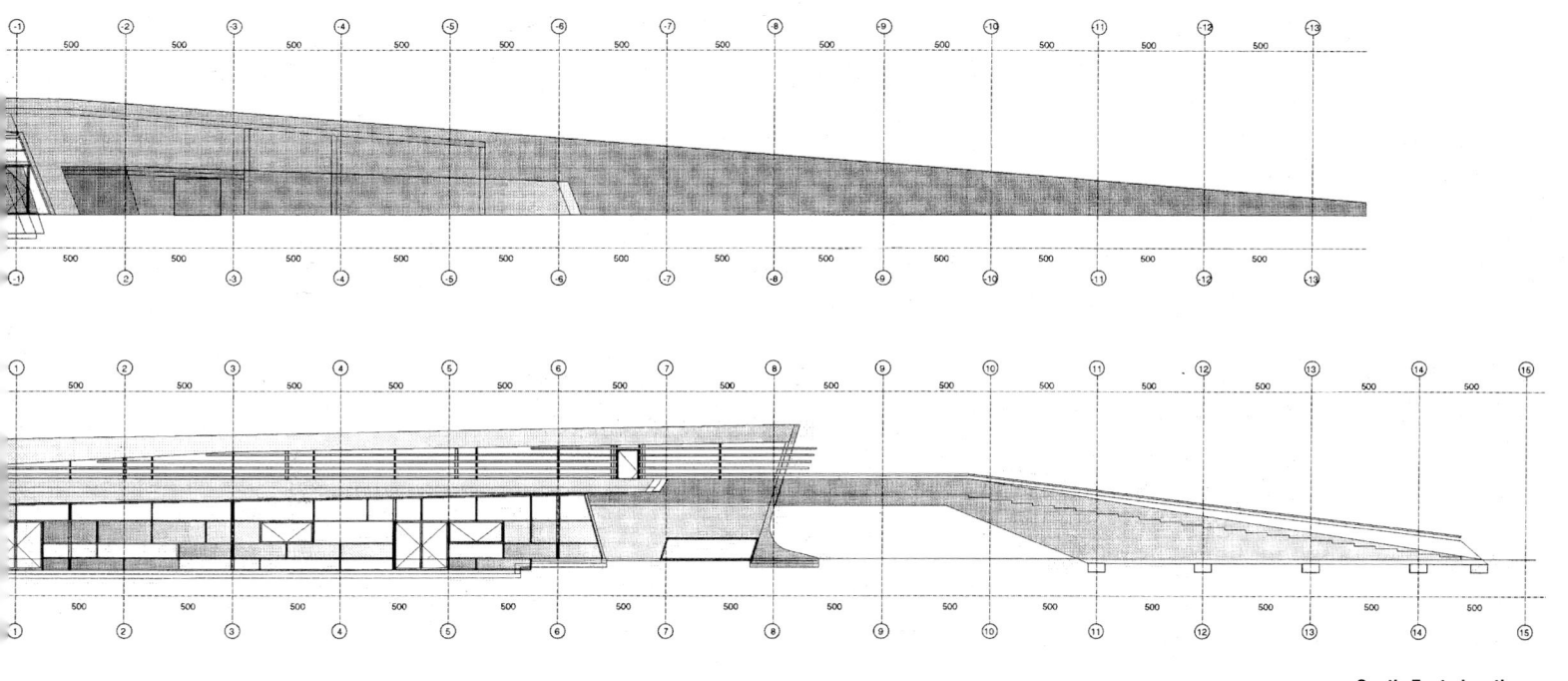

South-East elevation
Ansicht, Südosten

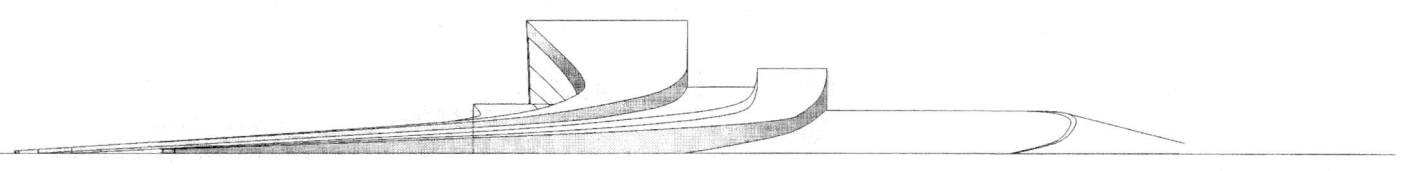

0 1 2   5   10 m

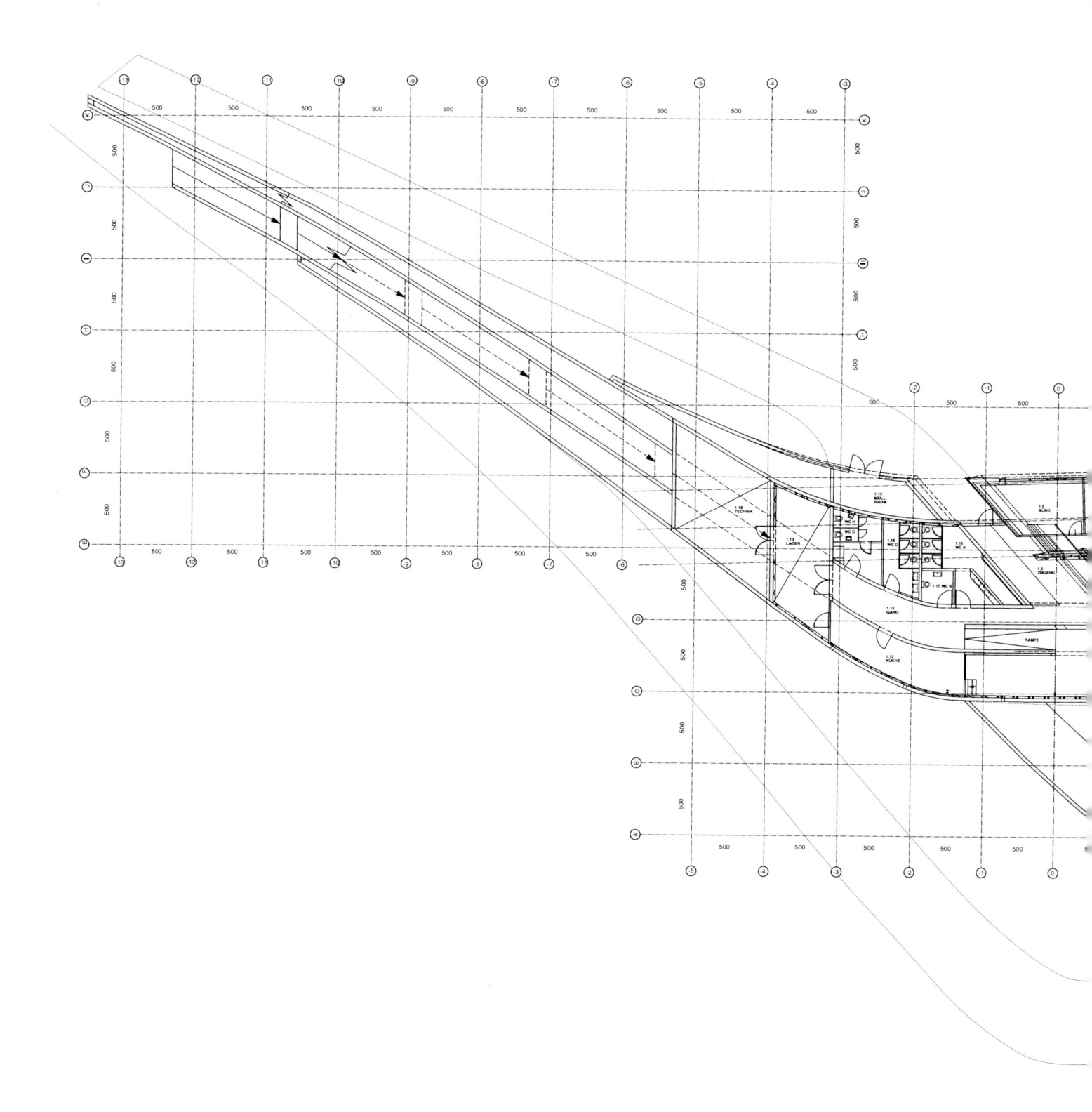

Ground floor
Erdgeschoß

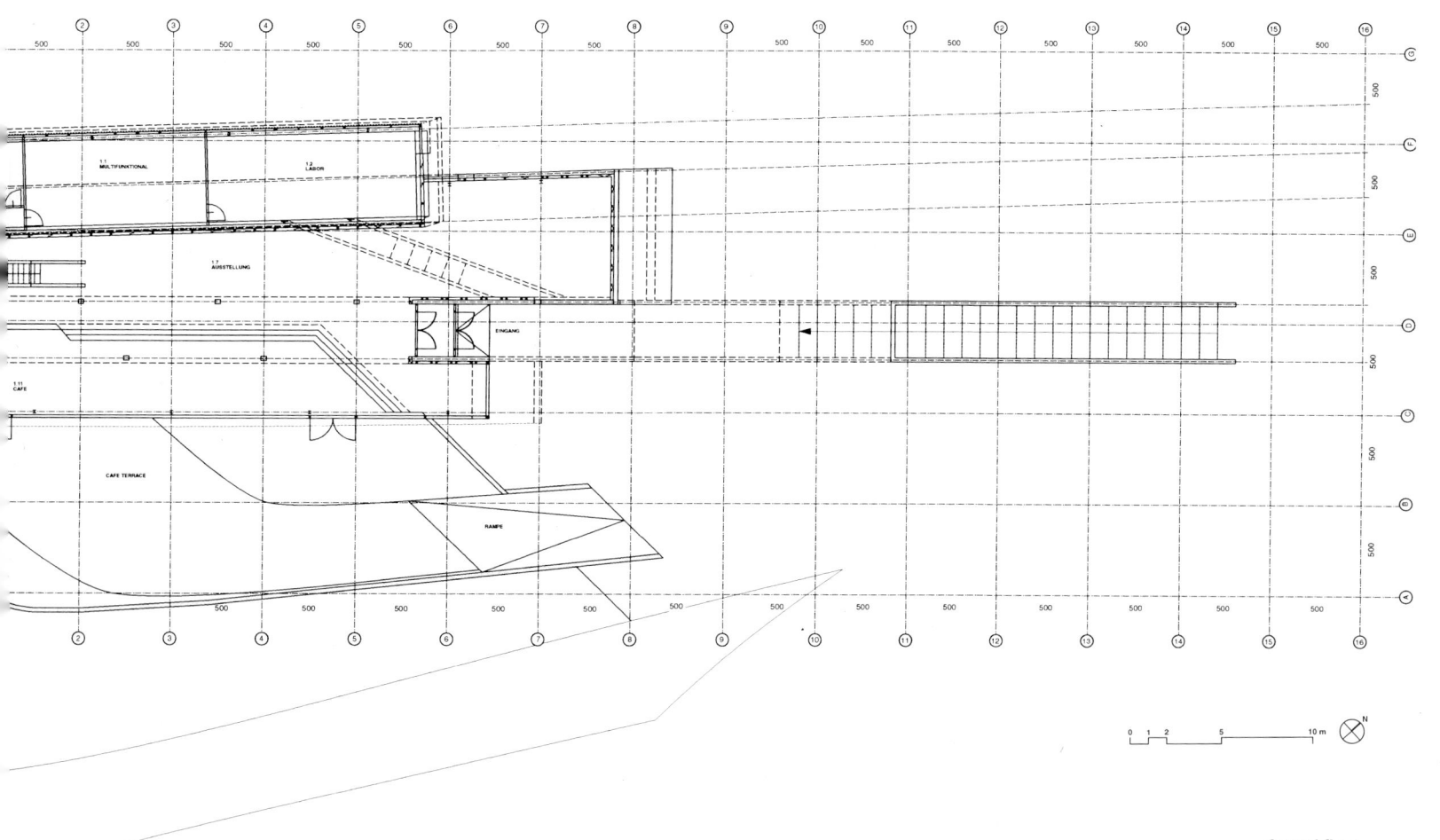

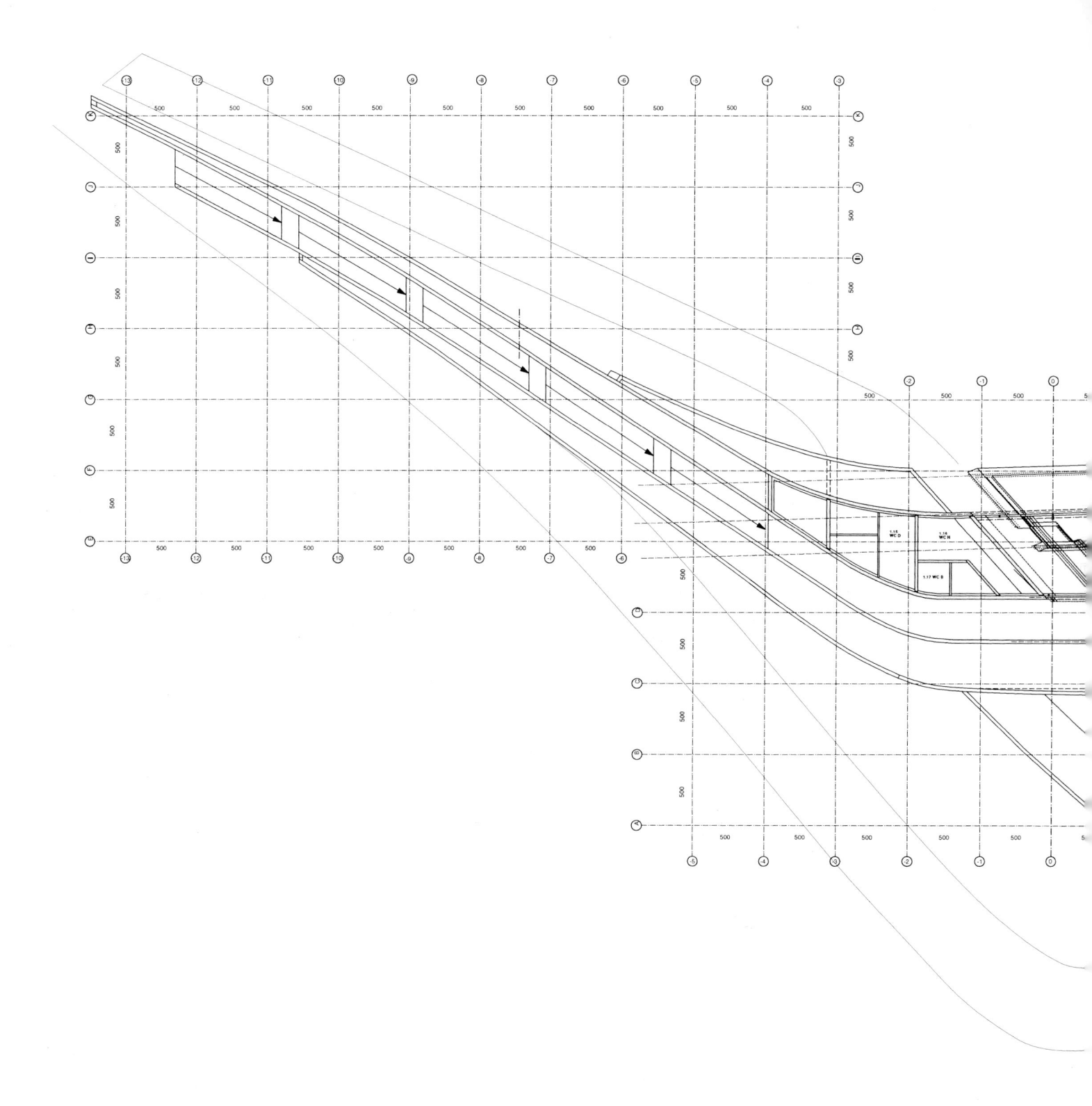

First floor
Obergeschoß

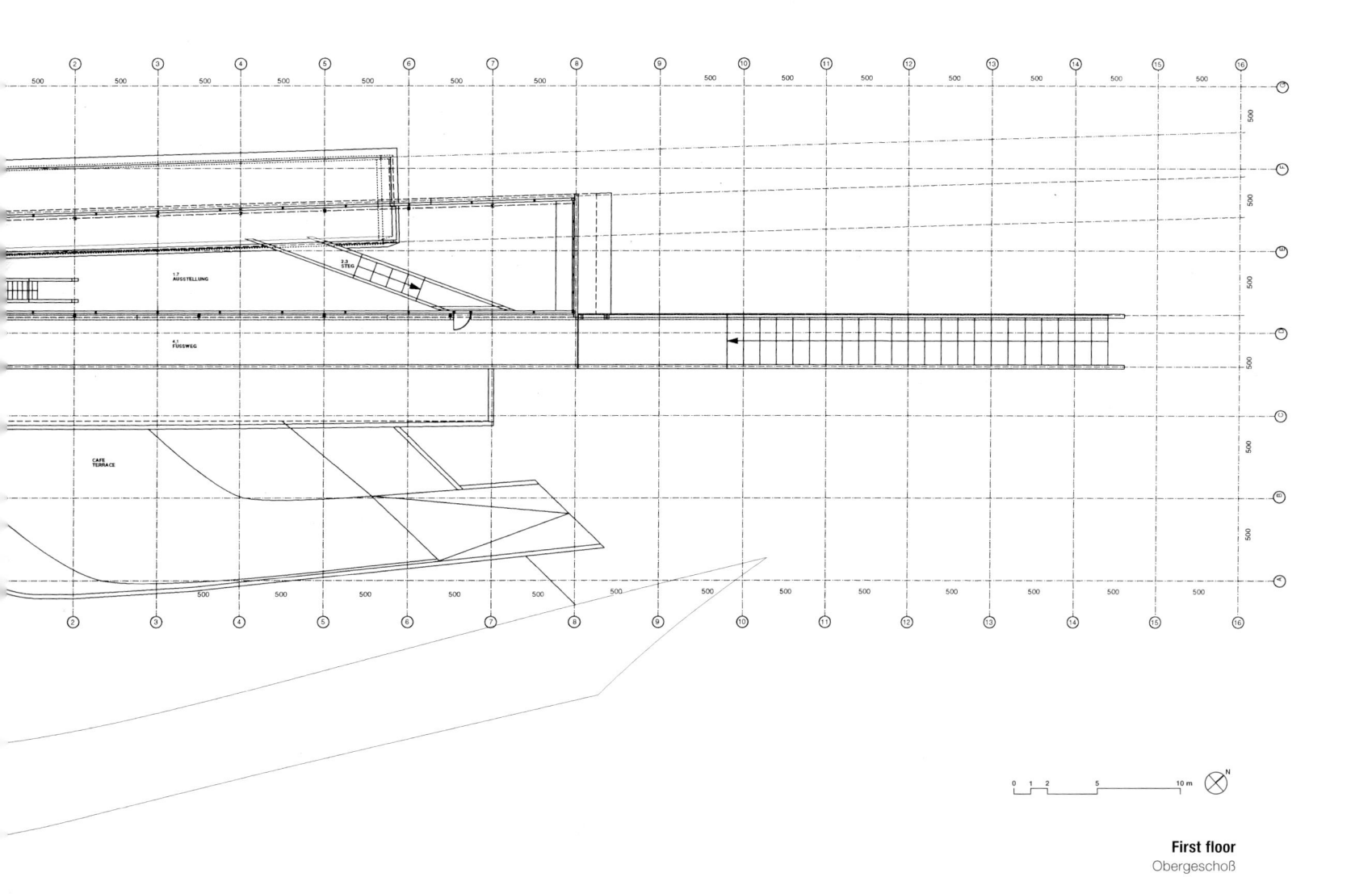

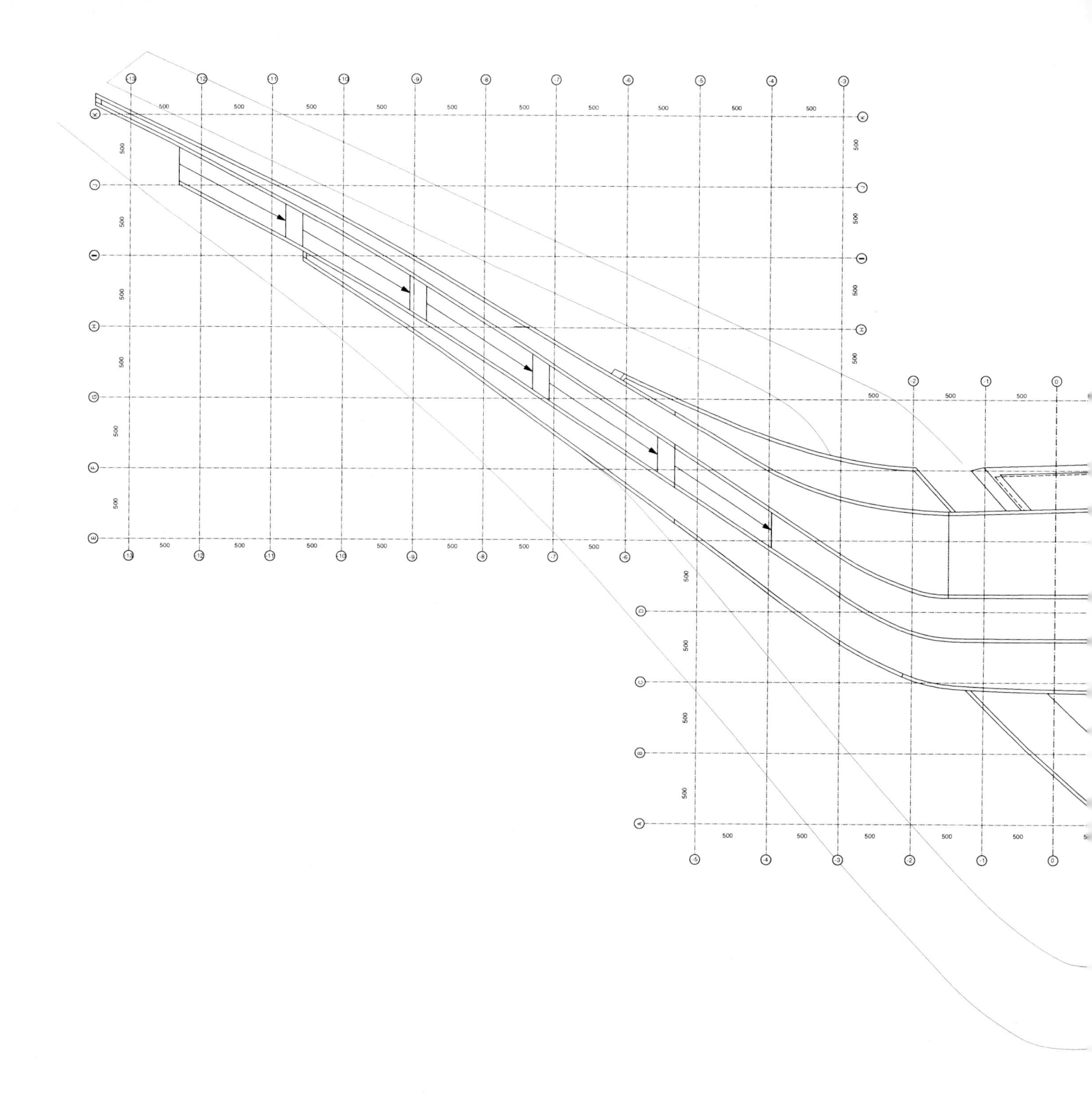

Roof plan
Dachaufsicht

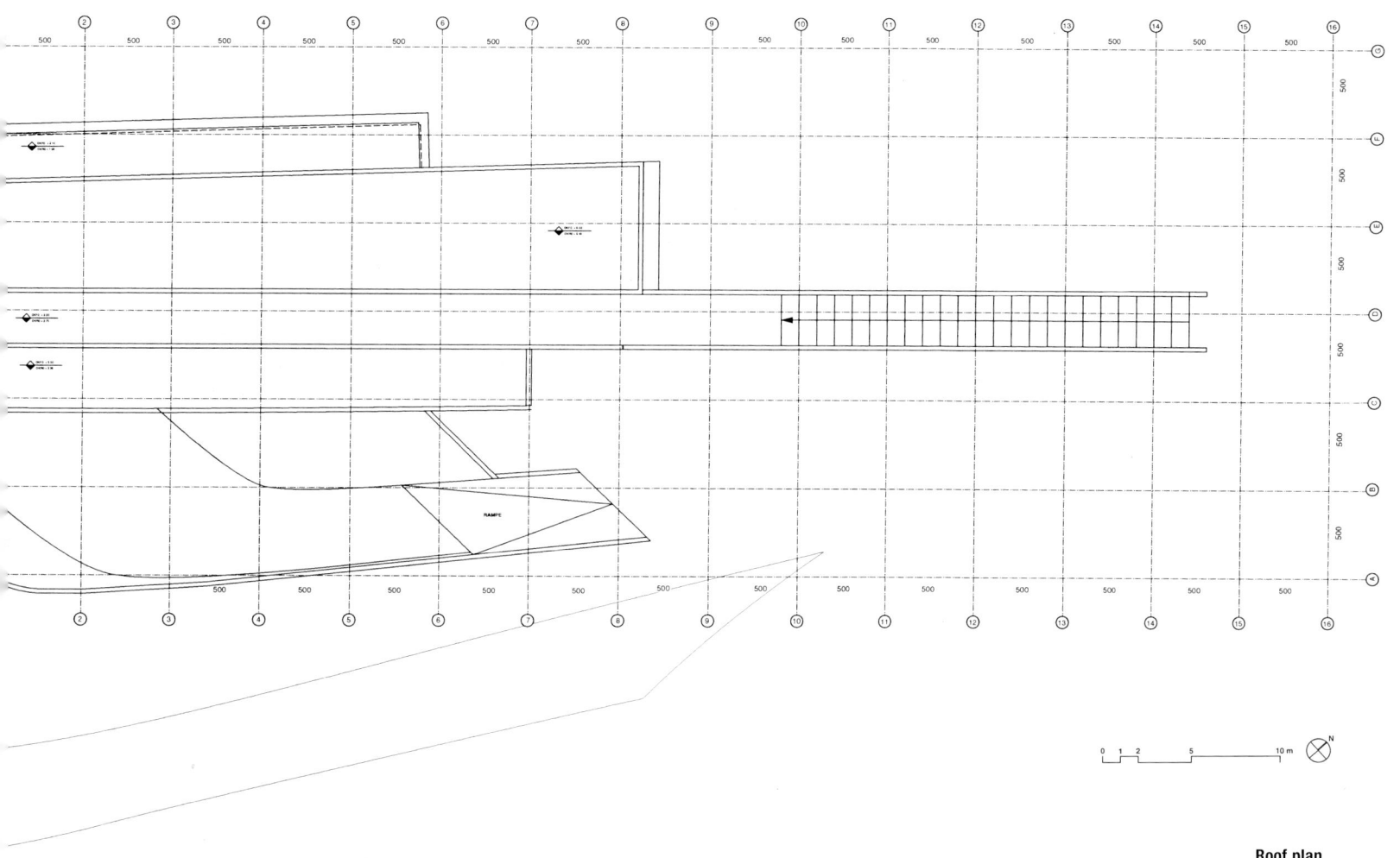

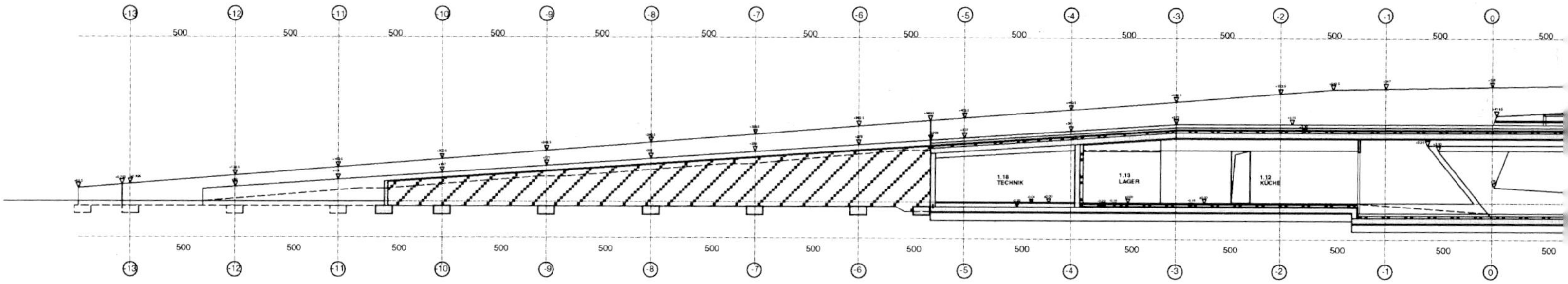
1.18 TECHNIK
1.13 LAGER
1.12 KÜCHE

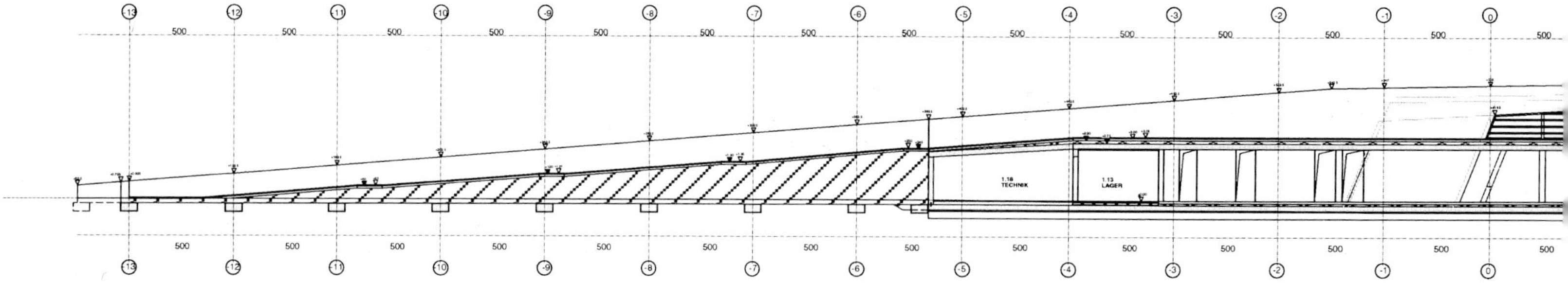
1.18 TECHNIK
1.13 LAGER

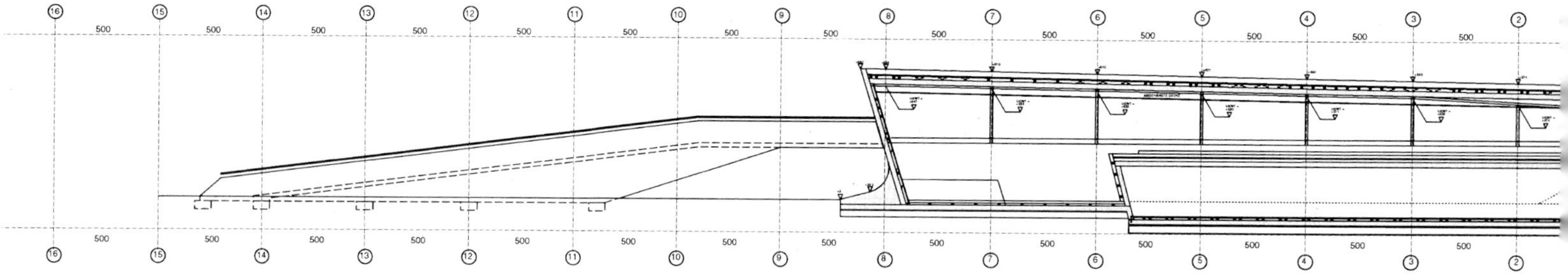

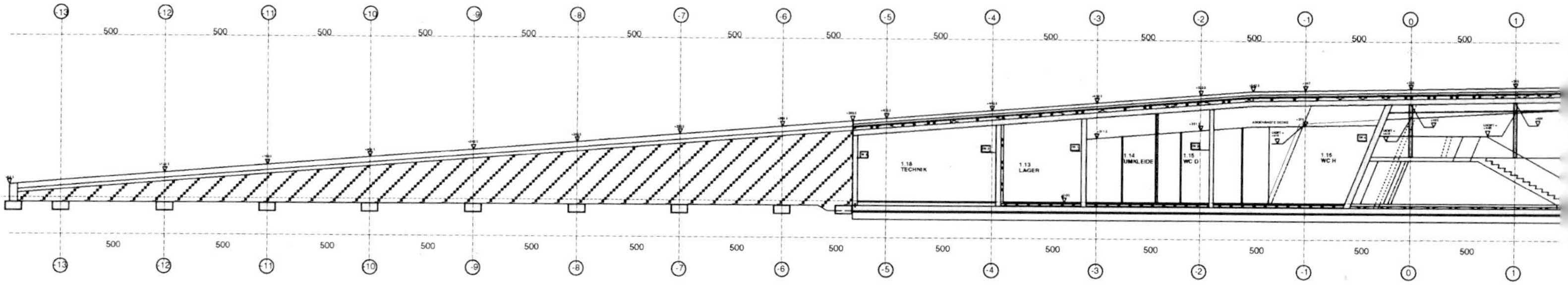
1.18 TECHNIK
1.13 LAGER
1.14 UMKLEIDE
1.15 WC D
1.16 WC H

Longitudinal sections
Längsschnitte

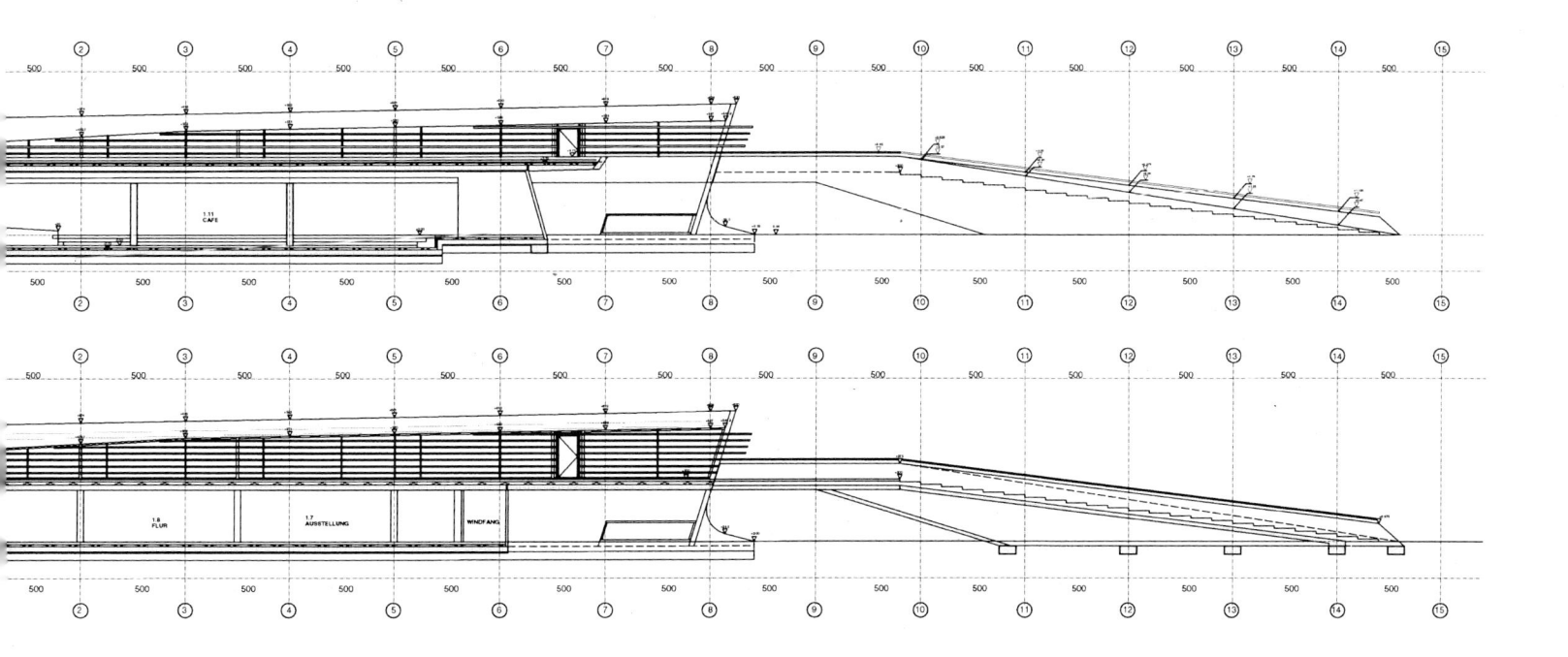

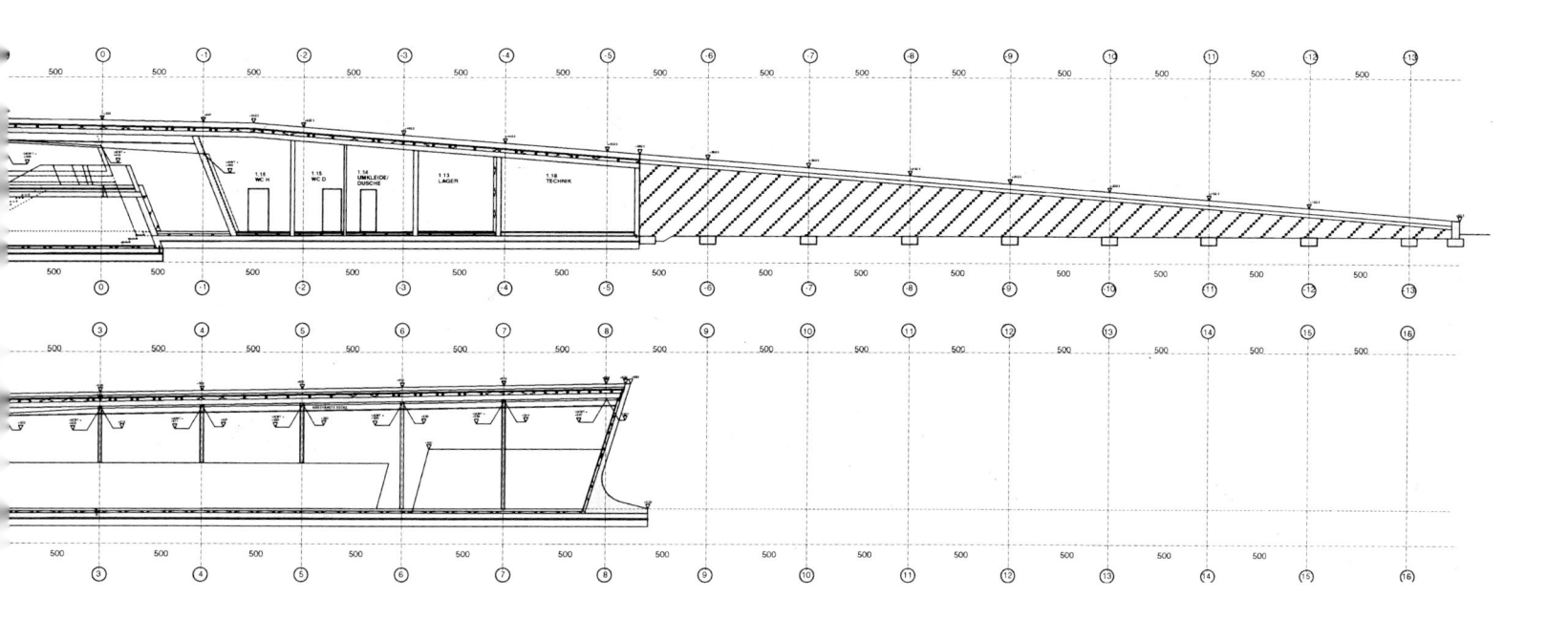

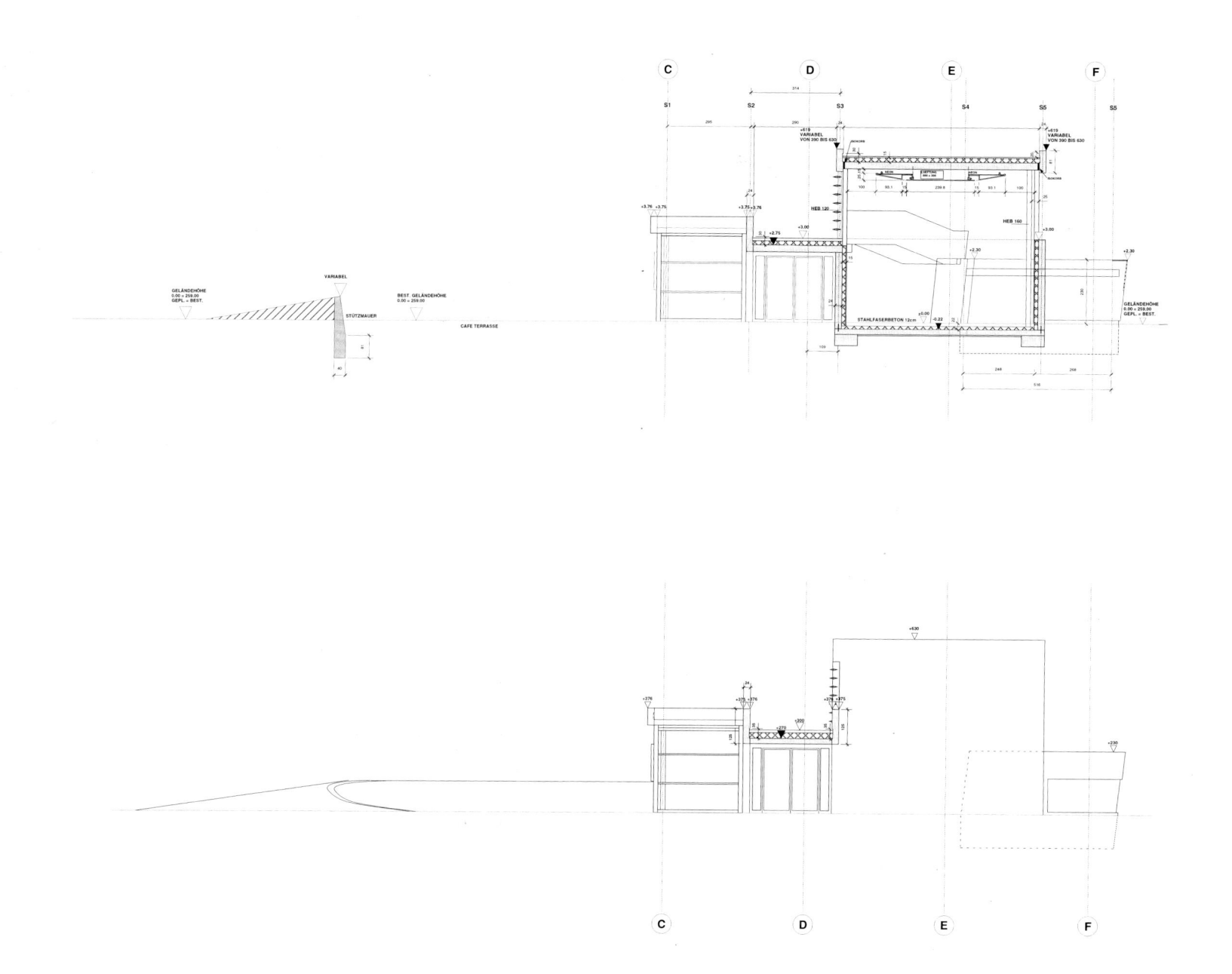

Cross sections
Querschnitte

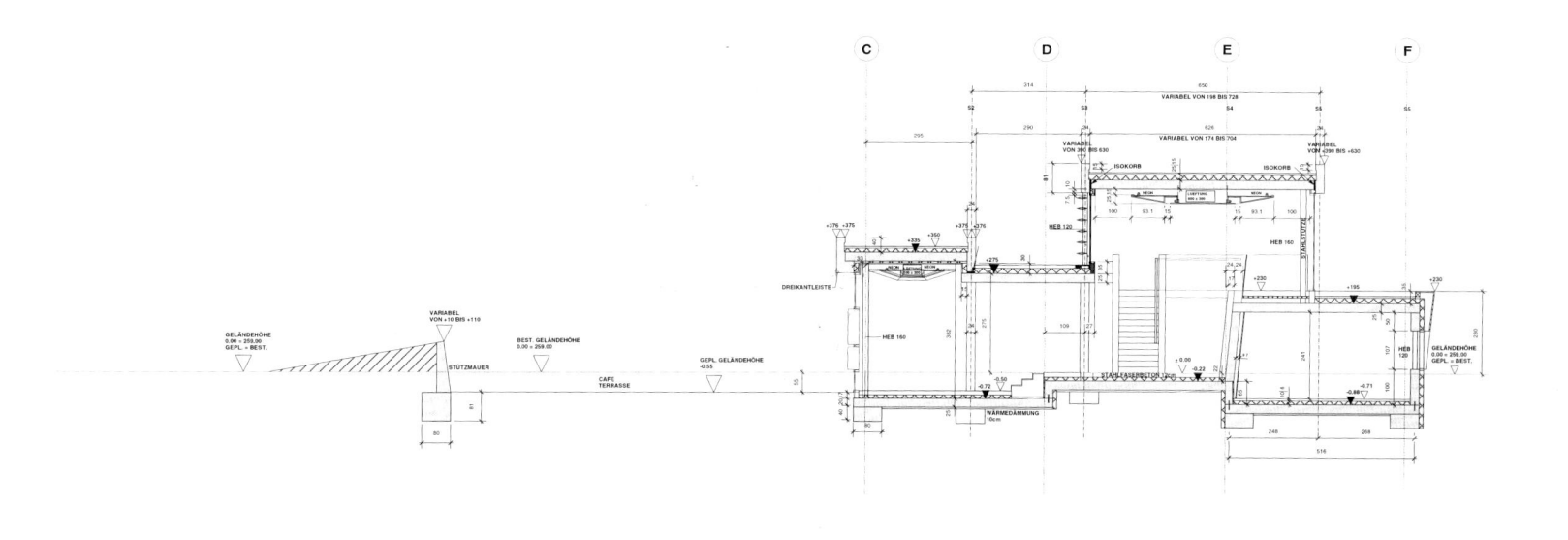

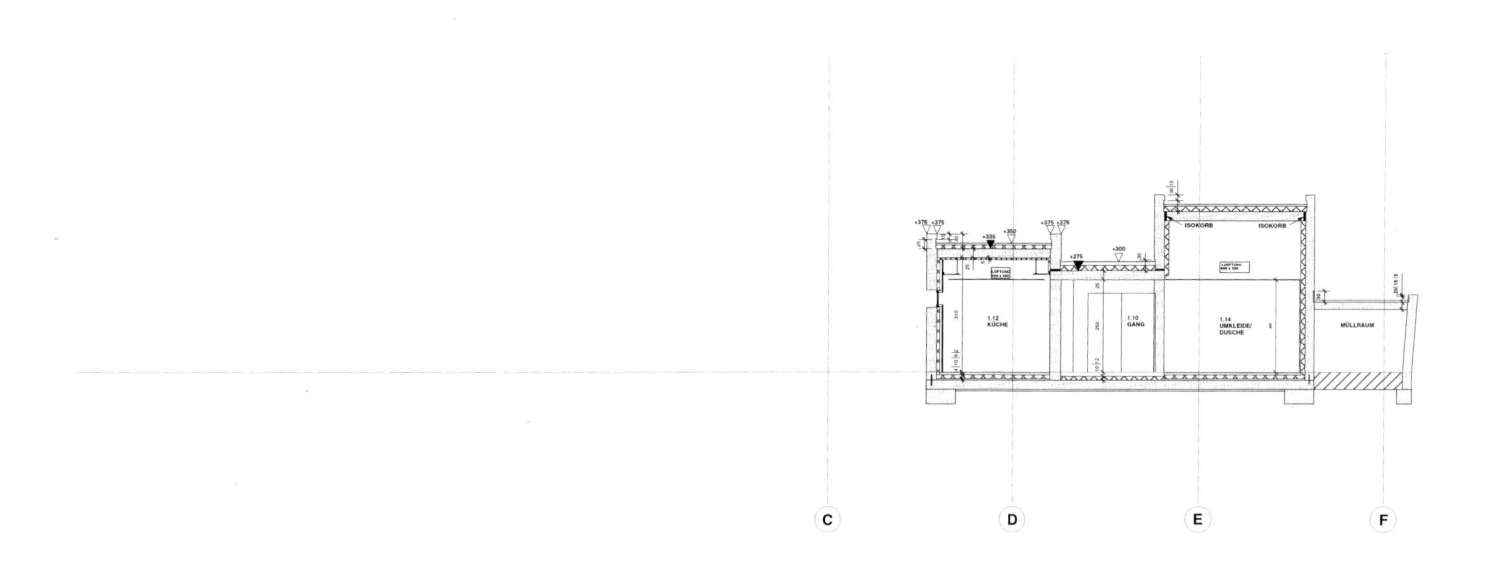

"The genuineness of a matter is the epitome of everything that can be handed down about it from its origin, from its material endurance up to its historic act of bearing witness."

(Walter Benjamin, *The Work of Art in the Age of Mechanical Reproduction*)

«Die Echtheit einer Sache ist der Inbegriff alles von Ursprung her an ihr Tradierbaren, von ihrer materiellen Dauer bis zu ihrer geschichtlichen Zeugenschaft.»

(Walter Benjamin, *Das Kunstwerk im Zeitalter seiner technischen Reproduzierbarkeit*)

Thoughts on the essence of being 1

The constructed building, whose character already has a transitory quality, went through a transition during the months of its construction and crossed a threshold during this process – from the virtual and universal to the here and now, that is to say, into a state of a material manifestation and thus into a historic witnessing. It has entered into the realm of experience. In this realm of experience many contexts can be found that are removed from purely verbal presentation, and yet in their entirety they constitute the essence of being in the here and now of the building. In the end, this refers to the entirety of the manifold phenomena accessible to sensual perception, even matters as simple as the unmistakable smell of fresh cement that sometimes fragranced the building site, or the symphony of the concrete mixers, drills and saws that now and then enveloped the building site in a many-voiced blanket of sound, but also the cool grace of reinforced steel covered with dew... The cinematic sequence of building site pictures reveals brief moments of growth in the form of still shots, and in its entirety it creates an atmospheric impression of the construction process.

Gedanken zum Sosein 1

Das Gebaute, welches schon von seiner Disposition her transitorischen Charakter aufweist, hat in den Monaten seines Entstehens selbst eine Transition durchlaufen und im Verlauf dieses Prozesses eine Schwelle überquert – vom Virtuellen, Universellen ins Hier und Jetzt, das heißt in einen Zustand materieller Gesetztheit und damit auch geschichtlicher Zeugenschaft. Das Gebaute ist in den Bereich der Erfahrung eingetreten. In diesem Bereich der Erfahrbarkeit sind viele Zusammenhänge angesiedelt, die sich der reinen verbalen Darstellung entziehen und doch in ihrer Gesamtheit das Sosein im Hier und Jetzt des Gebäudes ausmachen. Damit ist letztlich die Gesamtheit der mannigfaltigen Phänomene gemeint, welche den sinnlichen Wahrnehmungen zugänglich sind, auch so einfache Dinge wie der unverwechselbare Geruch frischen Zements, von dem die Baustelle bisweilen durchdrungen war, oder der Gesang der Betonrüttler, Bohrer und Sägen, die die Baustelle zeitweise mit einem vielstimmigen Klangteppich überzogen, aber auch die kühle Anmutung taubefeuchteter Armierungsstähle... Die filmische Sequenz von Baustellenphotos gibt standbildartig jeweils kurze Augenblicke des Wachstums preis und läßt in ihrer Gesamtheit einen atmosphärischen Eindruck vom Bauprozeß entstehen.

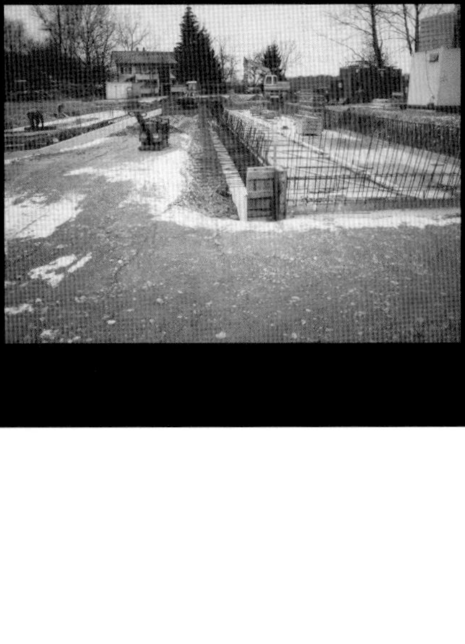
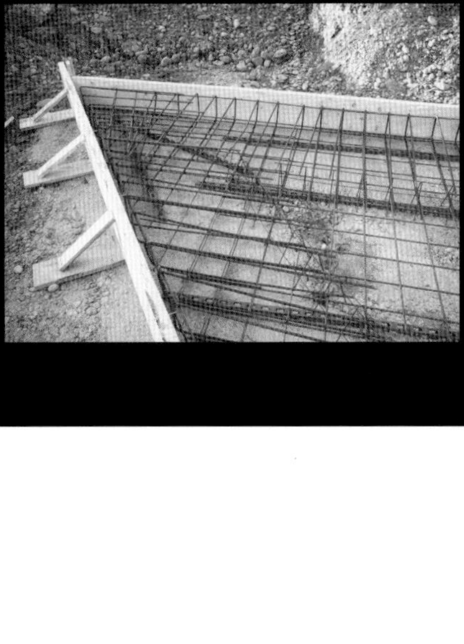
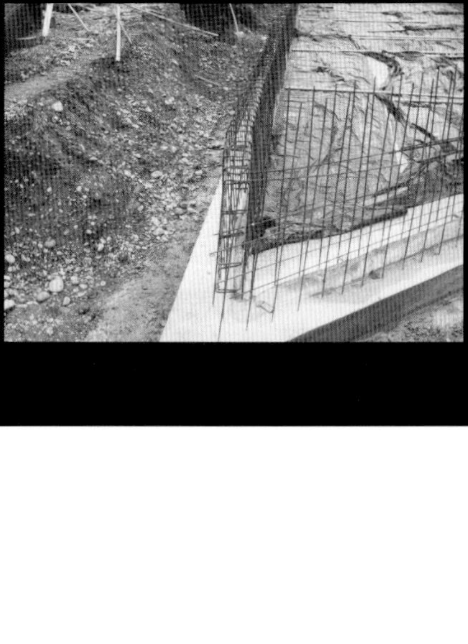
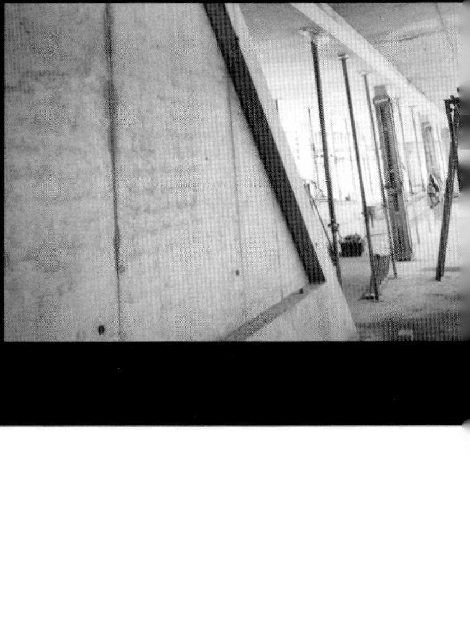

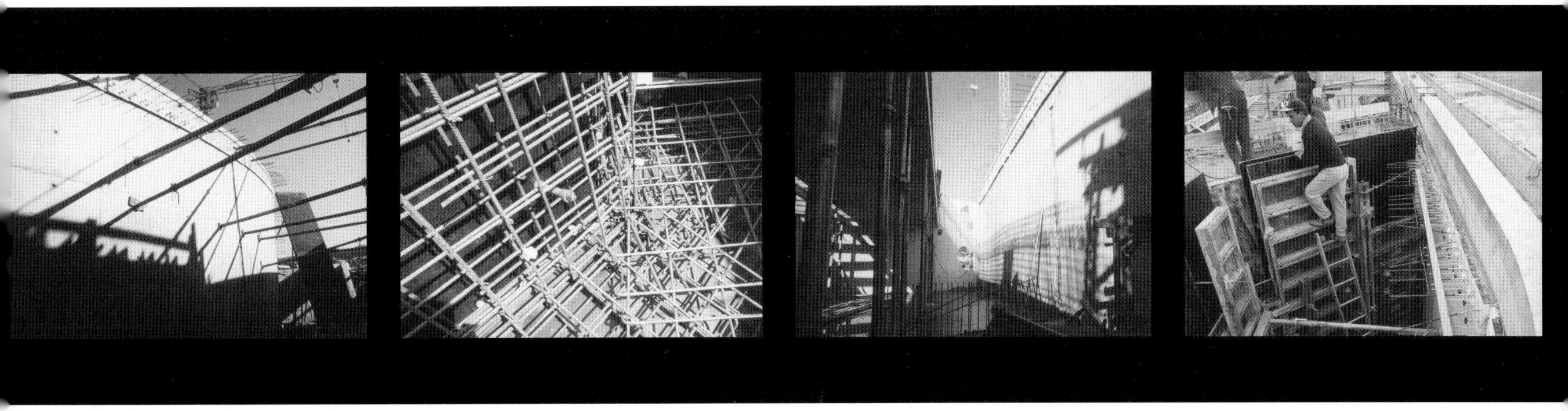

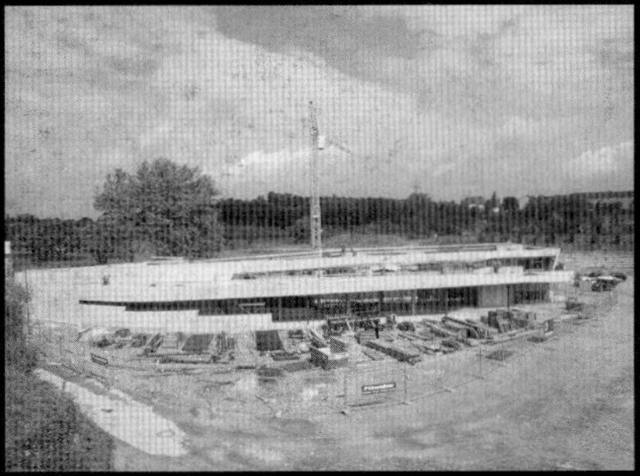
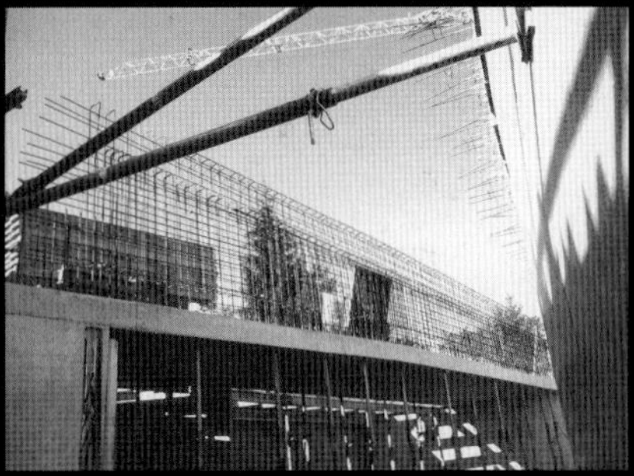
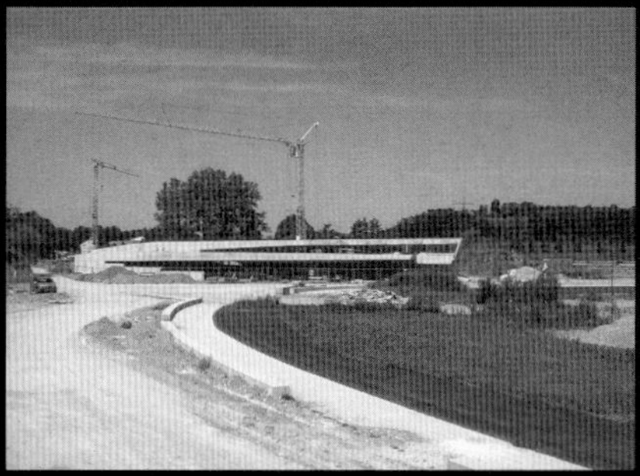
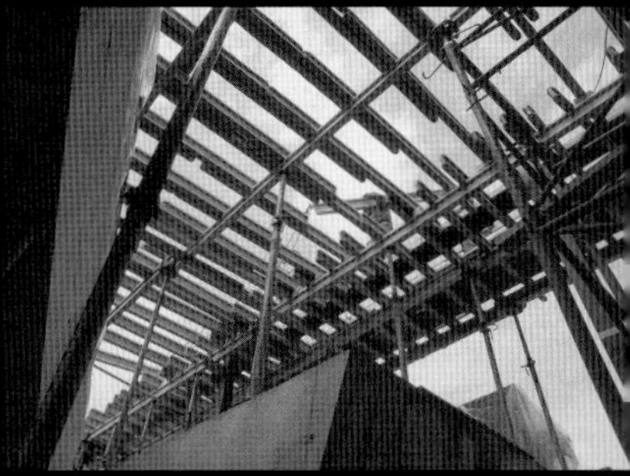

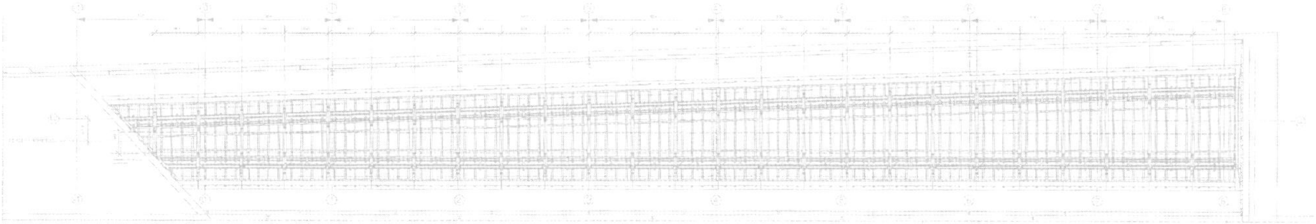

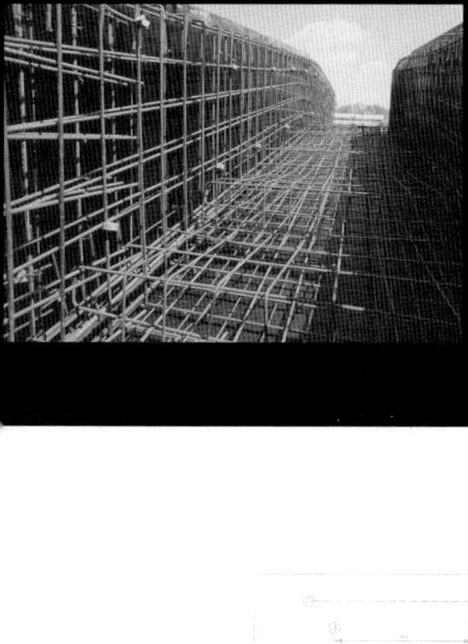

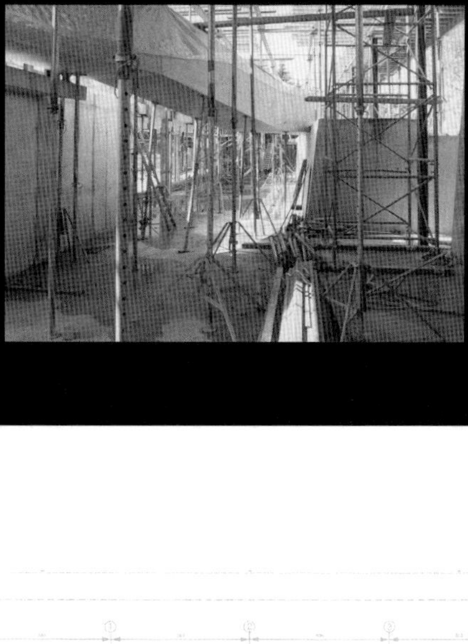

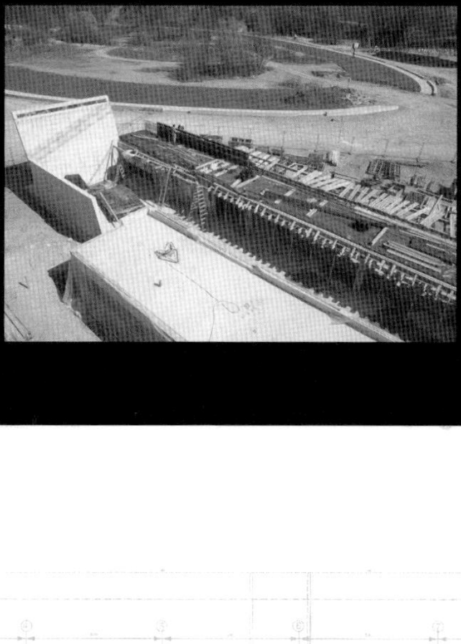

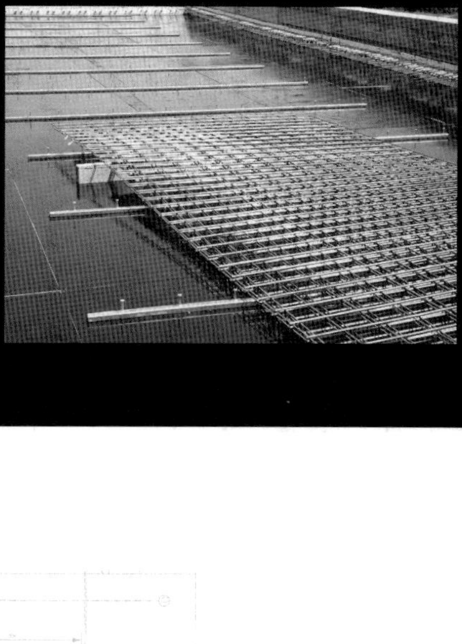

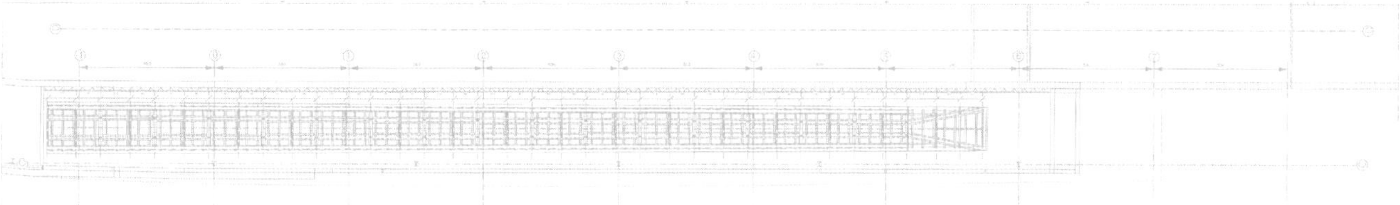

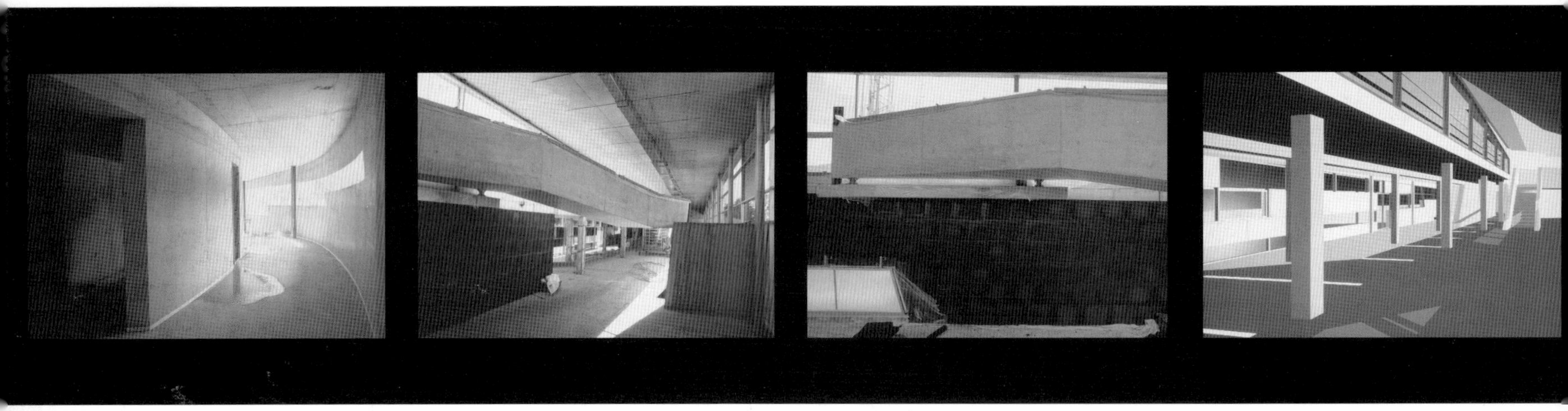

BEWEHRUNG DECKE TREPPE

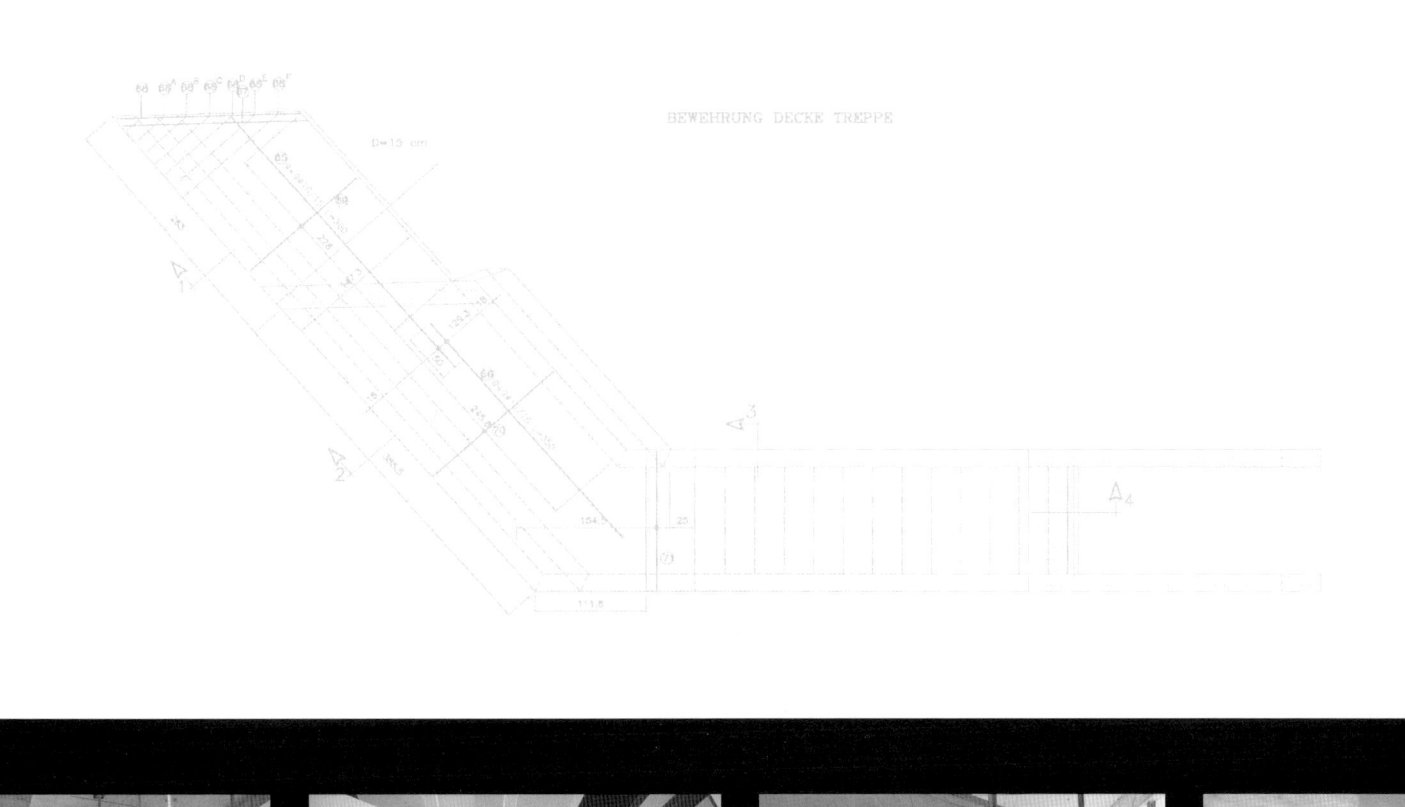

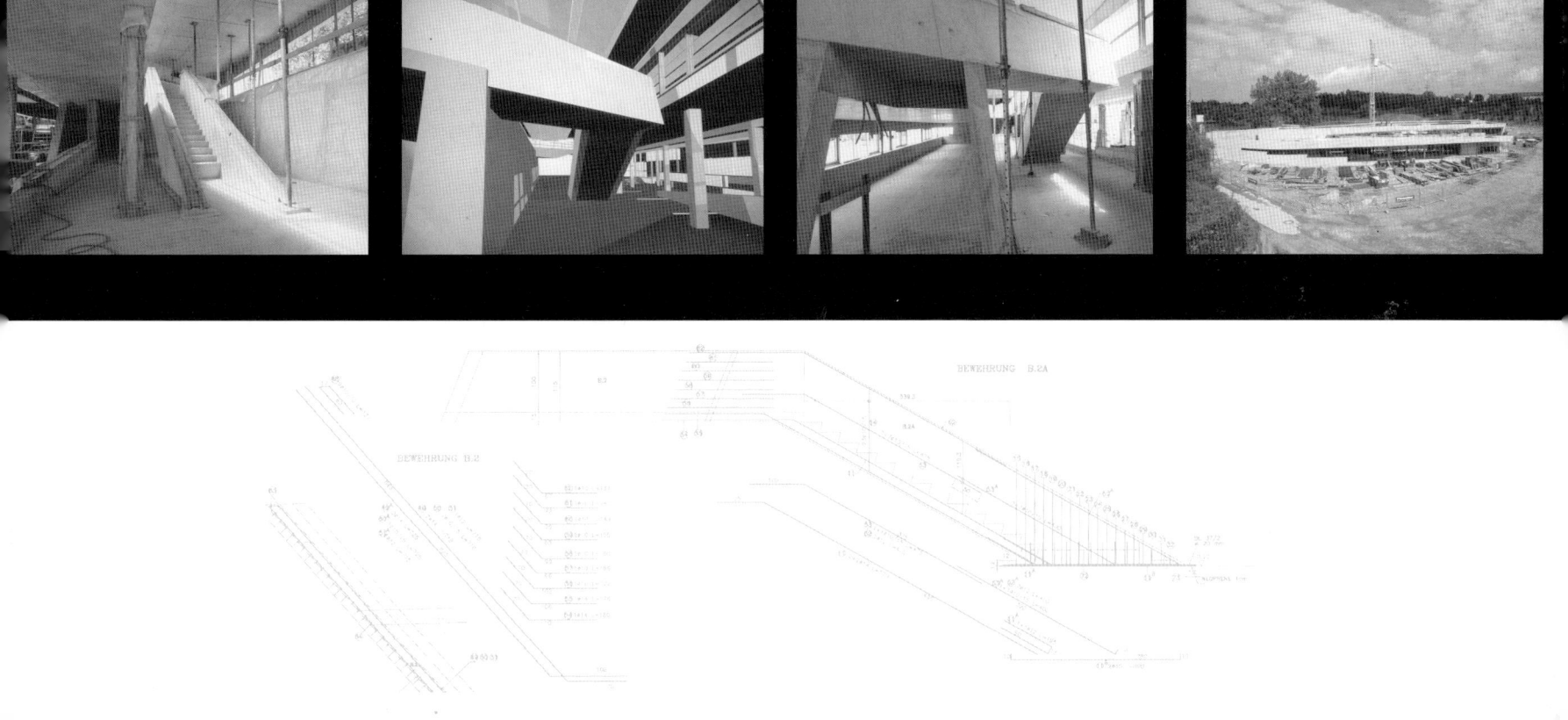

BEWEHRUNG B.2

BEWEHRUNG B.2A

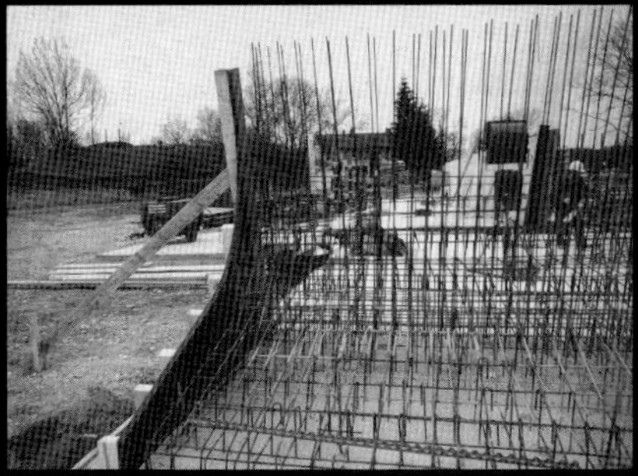

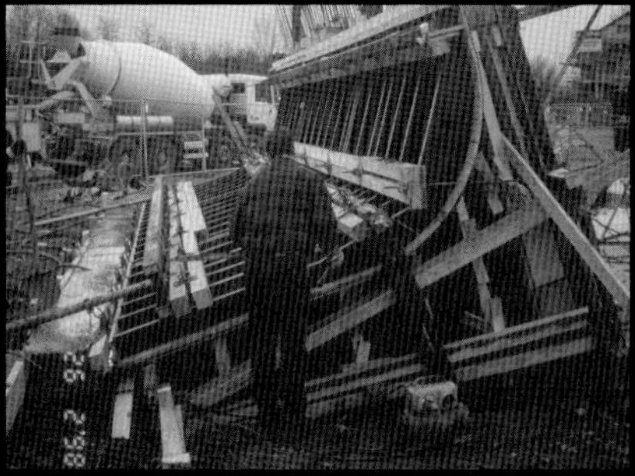

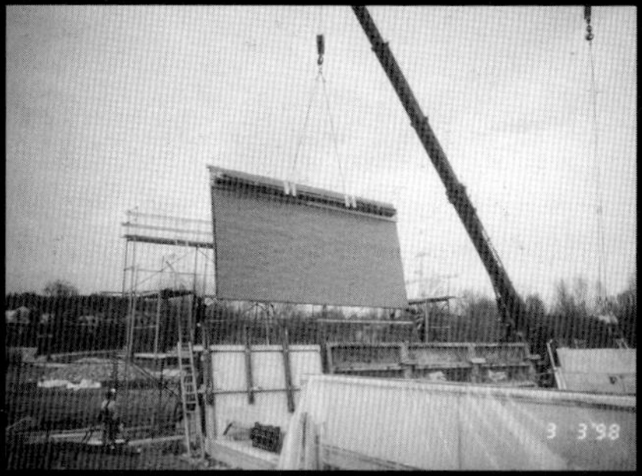
3 3'98

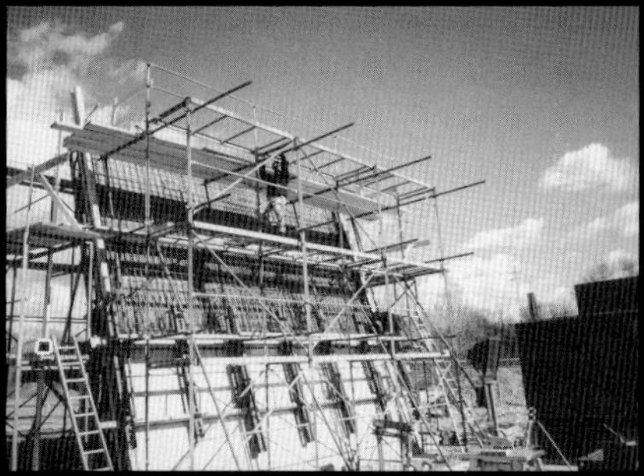

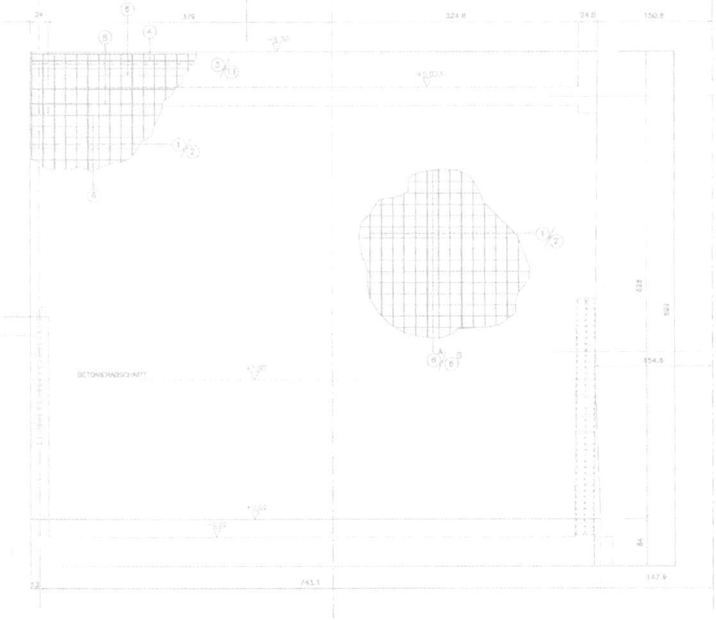

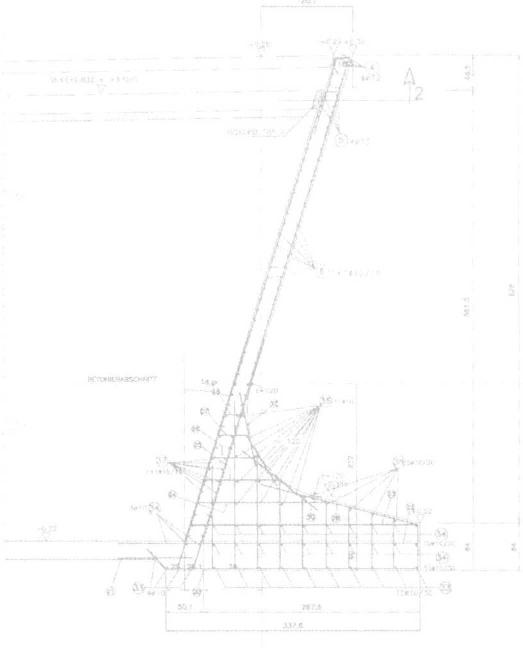

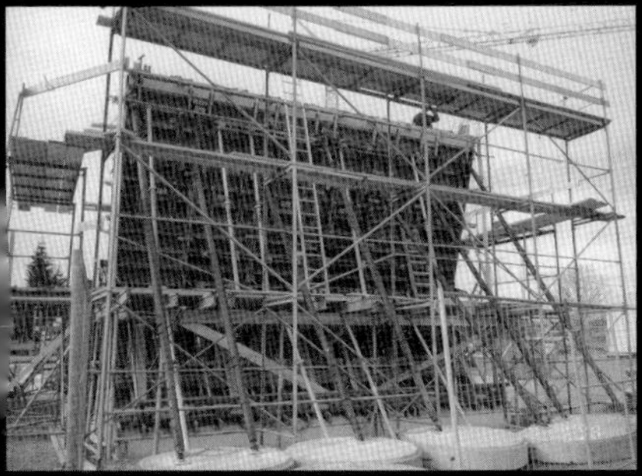

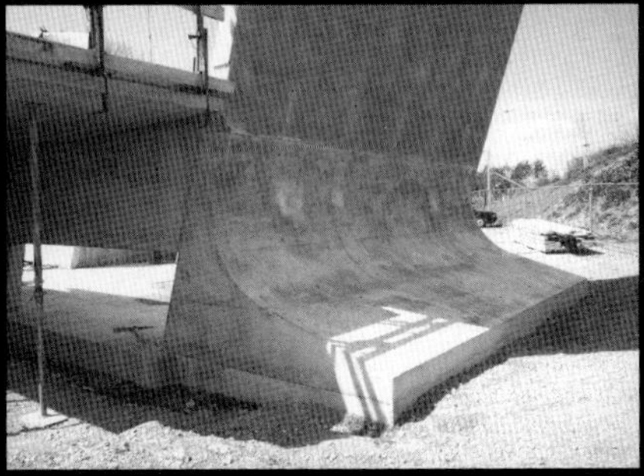

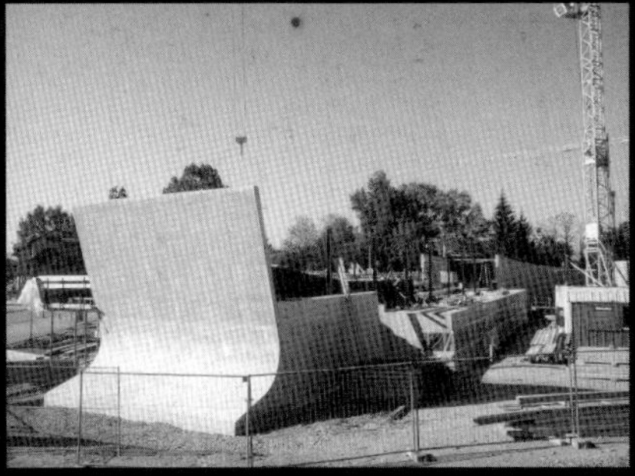

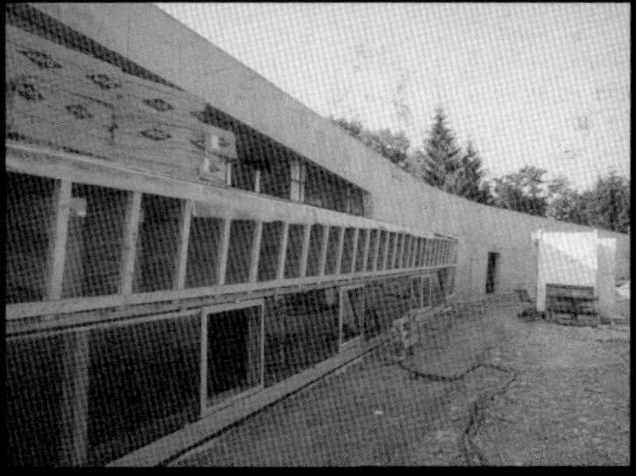

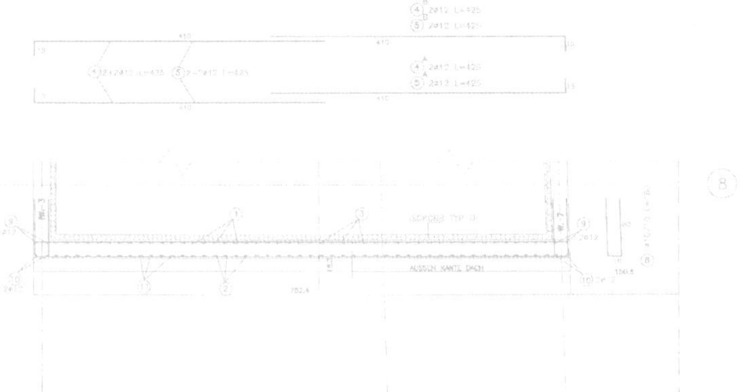

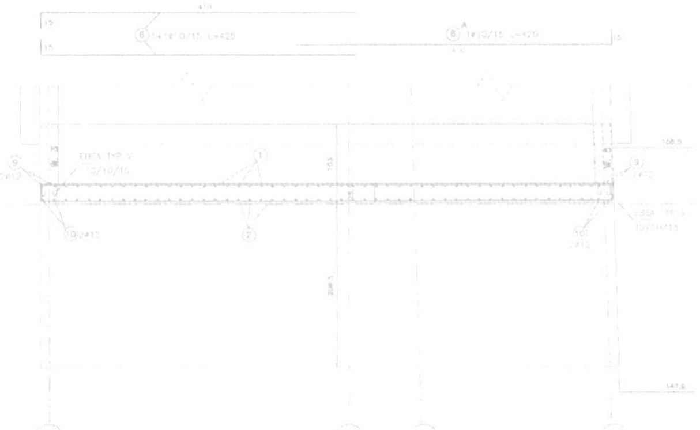

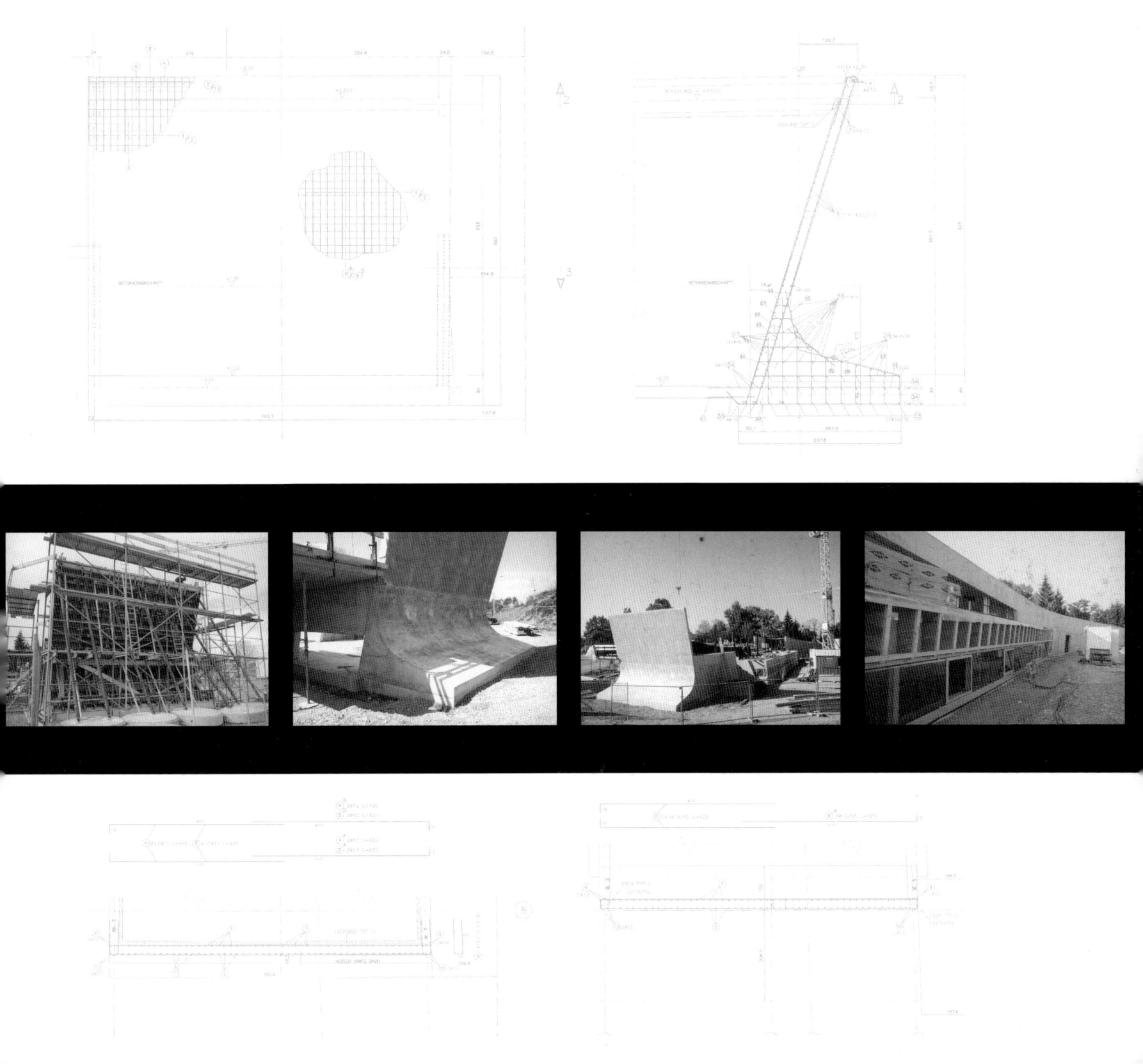

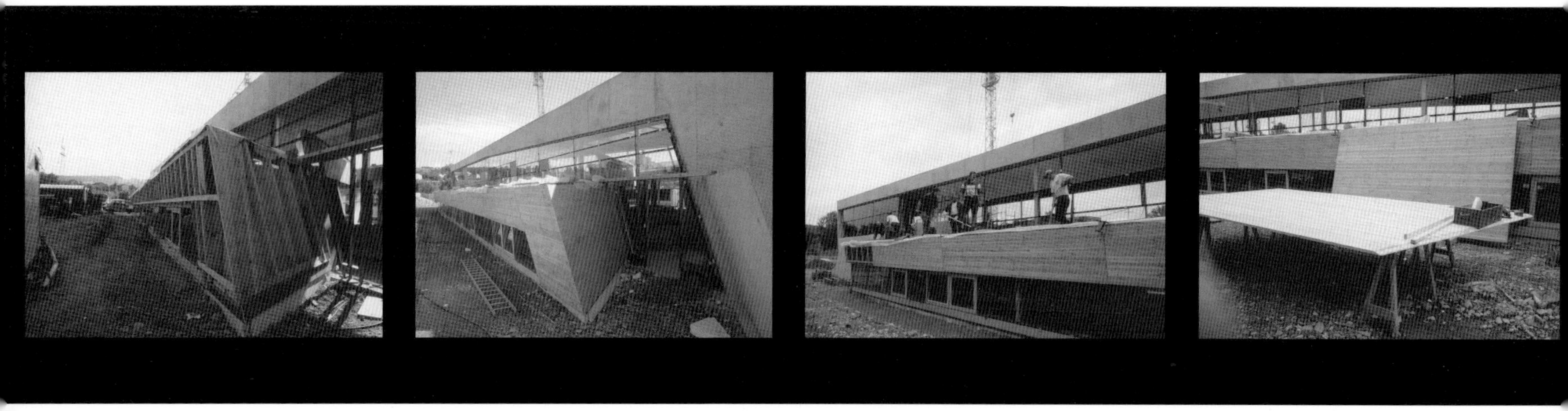

Thoughts on the essence of being 2

The building in the gravel pit is, when it comes to the configuration of the different volumes, a concrete structure, and it can only be thought of and realized as such. The fascination created in us by the building material, in situ concrete, is largely based on the fact that it reflects the conditions of its creation with a high degree of precision and thus grants the highest degree of authenticity. The skin, resembling thin foil, diametrically opposes the powerful materiality of concrete with its frailty. And it prohibits the slightest changes of the formwork surfaces, the weather conditions or the way it has been filled and condensed. With the curing process, petrified witnesses of the time come into being in time-lapse that again enter into a process of wear and erosion. The precision and unforgiving honesty of the expression required an analogous precision in the planning of the construction elements and in the preparation of the formwork and building materials, and it forced all participants in the building to proceed in a highly concentrated manner. An atmosphere of excited expectation came about in the separate work phases right up to the removal of the formwork and thus the unmasking of the finished form. The precision that was predetermined by the concrete engineer evoked an awareness of carefulness and precision in all the craftsworkers who followed. Building site parties created a balance and were a spoken expression of the atmosphere within which the building was evolving. During its creation it was already being inculcated with a lively spirit.

Gedanken zum Sosein 2

Das Gebäude in der Kiesgrube ist, so wie die Konfiguration der Baukörper ausgelegt ist, ein Betonbau und nur als solcher denkbar und realisierbar. Die Faszination, die der Baustoff Ortbeton auf uns ausübt, liegt zu einem großen Teil darin begründet, daß er mit höchster Präzision die Bedingungen seiner Entstehung widerspiegelt und mithin ein Höchstmaß an Authentizität gewährt. Die einer feinen Folie ähnliche Haut steht in ihrer Fragilität der kraftvollen Stofflichkeit des Betons diametral gegenüber und bannt die geringsten Veränderungen auf der Schaloberfläche ebenso wie die Witterungsbedingungen sowie die Art und Weise des Einfüllens und Verdichtens. Mit dem Abbinden entstehen gleichsam im Zeitraffer versteinerte Zeitzeugnisse, die ihrerseits nun in einen Prozeß von Abnutzung und Erosion eintreten. Die Präzision und unerbittliche Ehrlichkeit des Ausdruckes erforderte eine analoge Präzision im Planen der Konstruktionselemente und im Vorbereiten der Schal- und Baumaterialien und zwang alle am Bau Beteiligten zu konzentriertem Vorgehen. So entstand bei den einzelnen Arbeitsschritten eine Atmosphäre spannungsvoller Erwartung bis zum Ausschalen und damit dem Offenbarwerden der fertigen Form. Die Präzision, mit welcher die Betonbauer arbeiteten, erzeugte auch bei allen Nachfolgehandwerkern ein Bewußtsein für Sorgfalt und Genauigkeit. Baustellenfeste sorgten für Ausgleich und waren beredter Ausdruck für die Atmosphäre, in der das Gebäude aufwuchs. Bereits im Entstehen wurde ihm so ein lebendiger Geist gleichsam einverleibt.

70

71

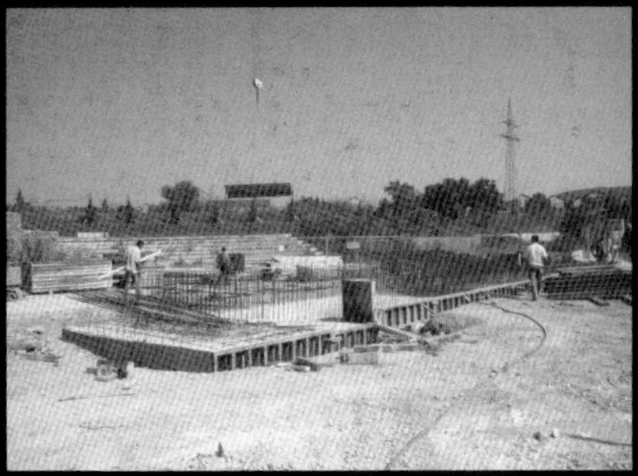

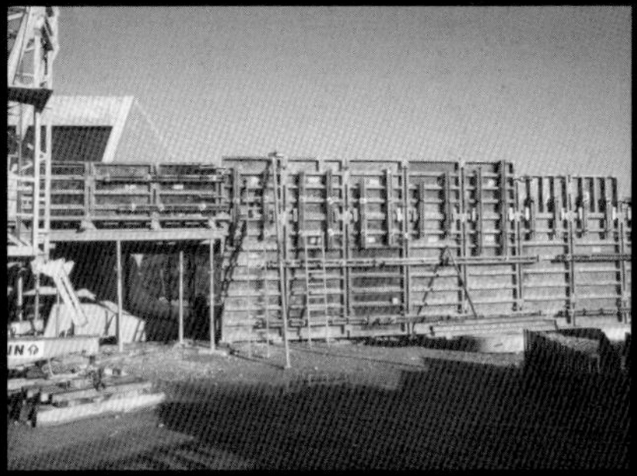

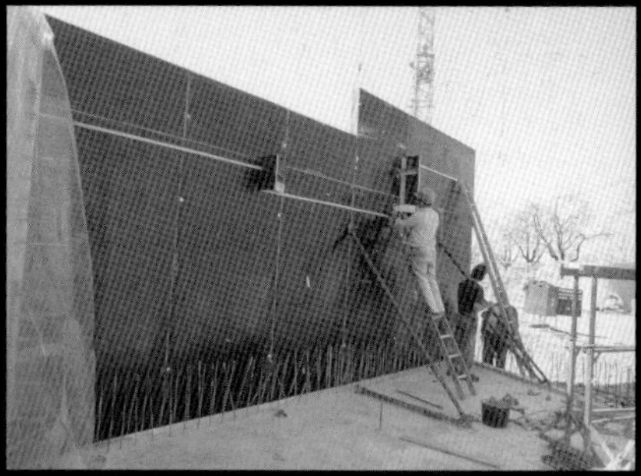

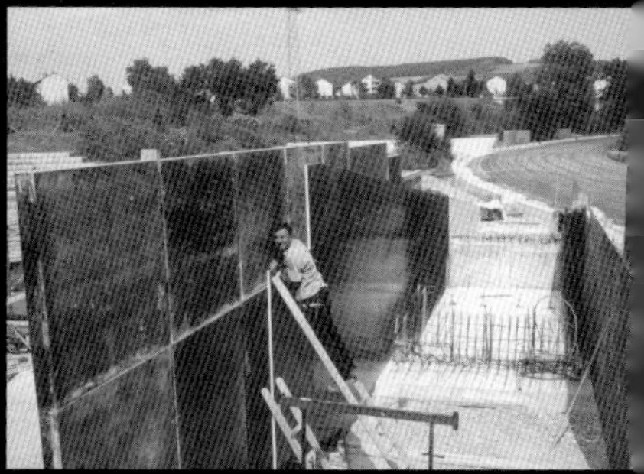

SCHNITT −3−

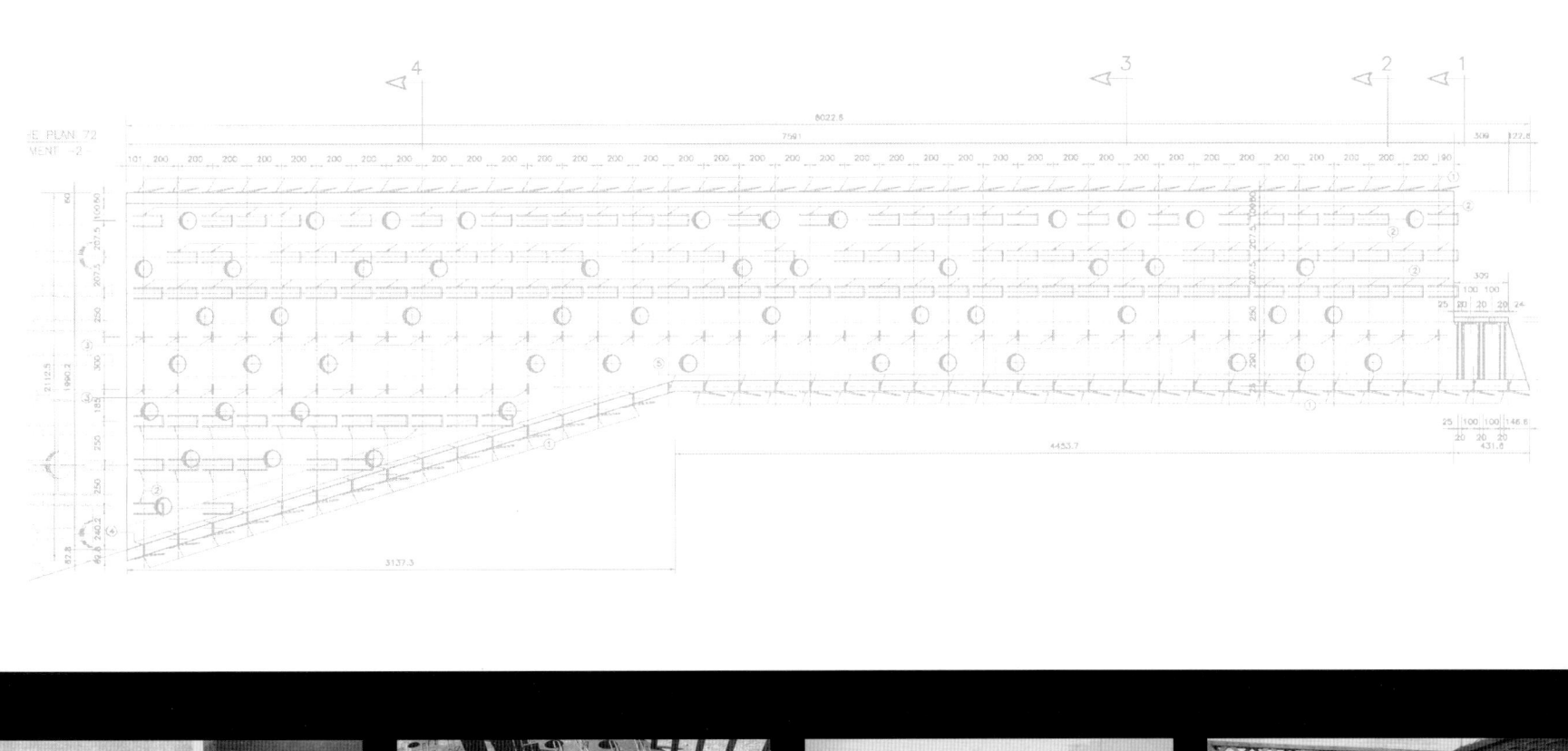

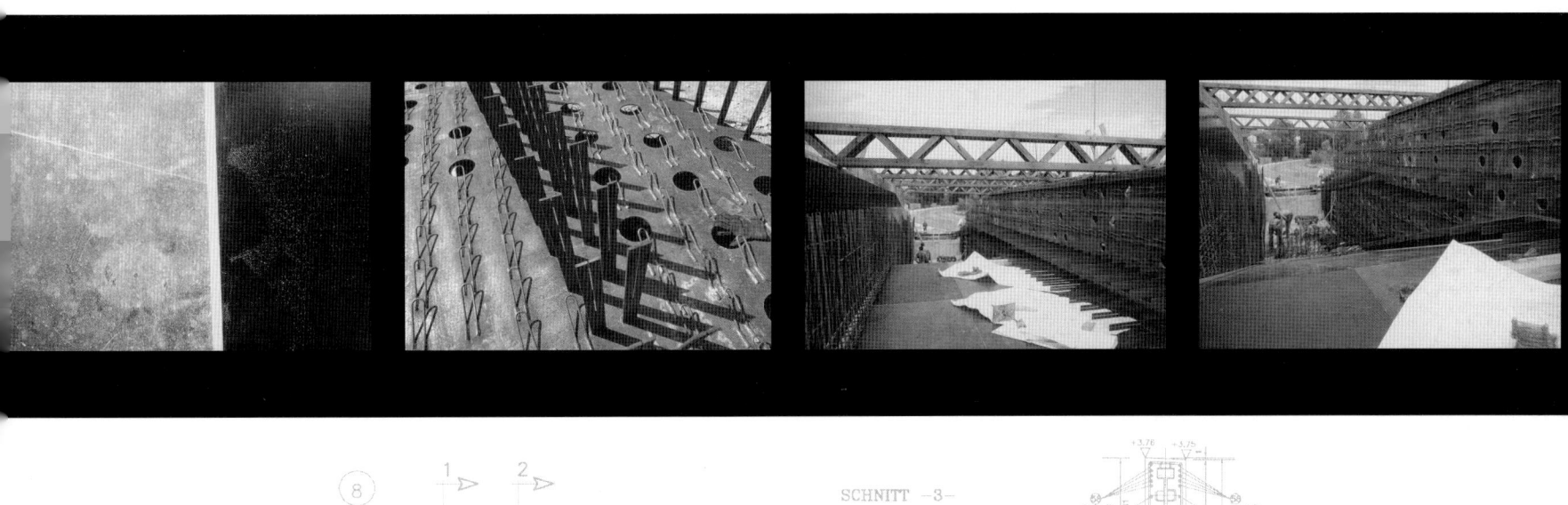

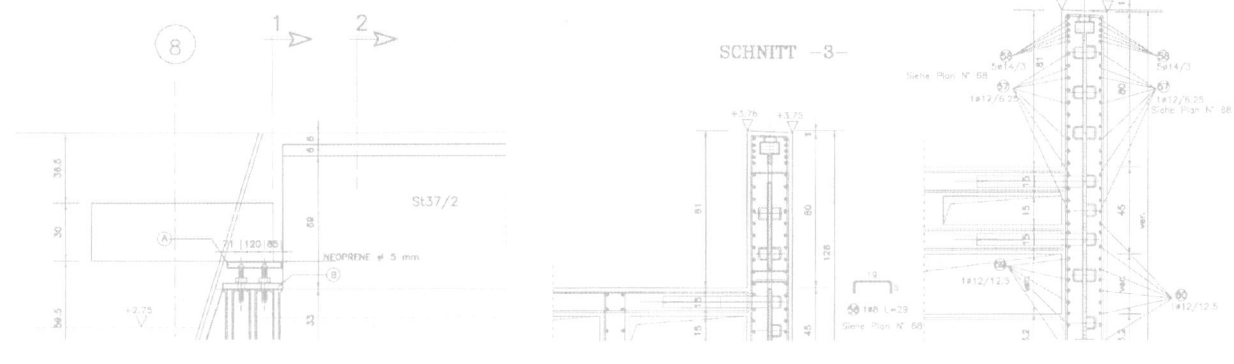

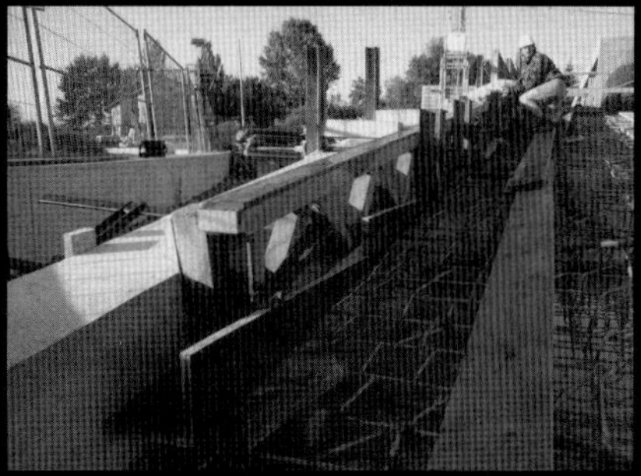
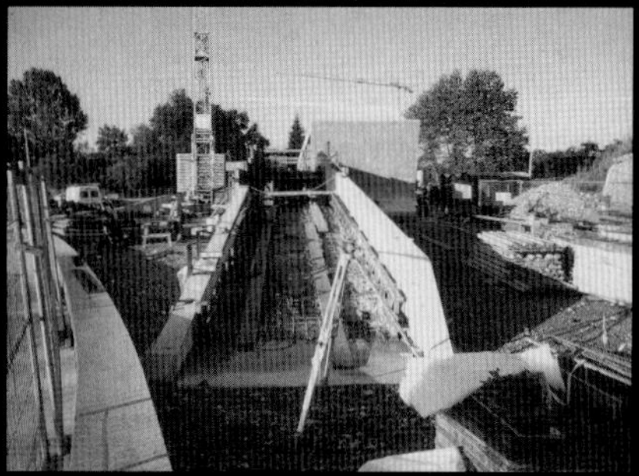
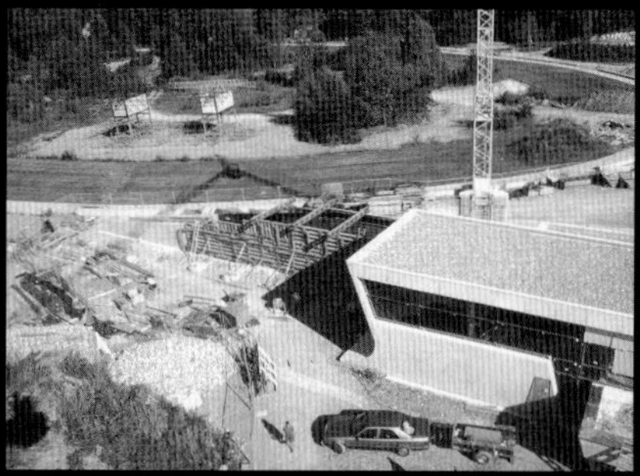
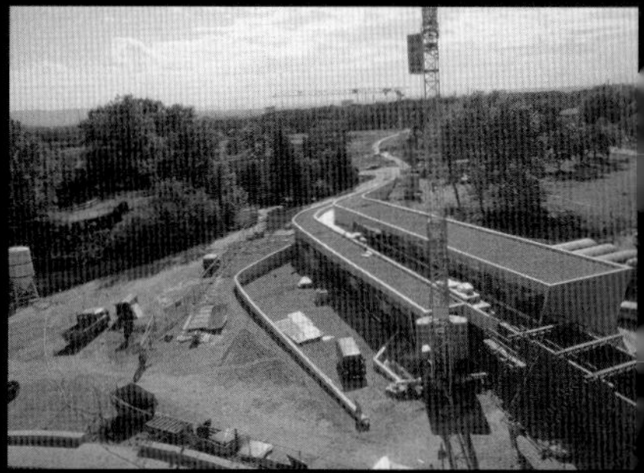

Thoughts on the essence of being 3

Hence the bride was carried literally from the realm of untouched virtuousness into the realm of reality – that is to say, into being – as is documented by the picture sequence. And, to stay with the root of the Latin virtus, it stood out in the material realm due to the virtuosity of the many. A classical threshold situation: plans, drawings and descriptions still had their effect, yet a physically dominated reality claimed its own right. At first, it did so discretely because one of the characteristics of this building is the fact that, as a result of the supporting system and building material, unlike a multistory building, it doesn't have a linear history of creation. Instead, the individual components (walls, wall-like supports, ceilings) were created separately in terms of time and space, similar to separate scenes in a movie production, and were joined only step by step. There still was a state of floating – to stay with the image of the carried bride – but physics has already begun to have an effect so as to later become a part of many additional facets of reality, whether economic, social or cultural, or components of other life processes that will be waiting for the building behind its doors.

mayer bährle

Gedanken zum Sosein 3

Die «Braut» wurde, wie in der Bildfolge dokumentiert, aus dem Virtuellen, d. h. wörtlich auch aus dem Bereich der unberührten Tugendhaftigkeit, in den Bereich des Wirklichen, also ins Leben, hinübergetragen. Sie wurde (um beim lateinischen Wortstamm «virtus» zu bleiben) durch die Virtuosität vieler Mitbeteiligter im Stofflichen abgesetzt. Eine klassische Schwellensituation: noch wirkten Pläne, Zeichnungen und Beschreibungen, aber schon forderte eine zunächst physikalisch dominierte Wirklichkeit ihr Recht ein. Zunächst punktuell, denn eine Eigenart dieses Baues ist die aus dem Baumaterial und dem Tragsystem resultierende Tatsache, daß er, anders als beispielsweise ein Geschoßbau, keine lineare Entstehungsgeschichte hat, sondern die Teile – Wände, wandartige Träger, Decken – vielmehr wie einzelne Szenen bei filmischen Produktionsvorgängen zeitlich und räumlich völlig getrennt entstanden und erst allmählich zusammengefügt wurden. Noch war, um beim Bild der getragenen Braut zu bleiben, ein Schwebezustand gegeben, aber die Physik hat mit ihrer Einwirkung bereits begonnen, um wiederum später selbst ein Teilaspekt vieler weiterer Wirklichkeitsfacetten zu werden, seien sie ökonomischer, sozialer, kultureller Art oder Bestandteile jener Lebensvorgänge, die das Gebäude hinter der Tür erwarten werden.

mayer bährle

The Perfection of Modernism

The Architect Zaha Hadid and her Visitors' Pavilion at the Gardening Show in Weil am Rhein

Robert Musil once said that great architecture could only be created if there was something to be glorified. Modernism posed the ultimate challenge to this notion, yet architecture unfolded with incredible splendor and fantasy in at least one period of this century, when during World War I, the European monarchies began to falter, and when Central Europe was filled with republican and social revolutionary hope after 1918. In Berlin, Vienna, Prague, Budapest and Moscow, an entire generation of young architects lived in a feverish dream of profane vocational visions and experiences of religious awakening. The master builders raved about the return of the emancipated human being into his natural condition of original sensuality, creating phantasmagoric caves and building mountains, "Wolkenbügel" and flying cities as symbols of community and temples of triumph to a freed people.

At the root of this fury that changed society was a new spiritual and educational approach to art which Gottfried Benn tried to sketch out in the fateful year of 1933 in an overheated verbal staccato: "Futurism as a style, also called Cubism, in Germany mainly called Expressionism, versatile in its empirical variation, uniform

Die Vollendung der Moderne

Die Architektin Zaha Hadid und ihr Besucherpavillon auf der Landesgartenschau in Weil am Rhein

Große Architektur, meinte einmal Robert Musil, entstehe nur, wenn es etwas zu verherrlichen gebe, was aber in der Moderne nicht mehr gelinge. Doch zumindest einmal in diesem Jahrhundert hat die Architektur eine ungeheure Pracht und Phantasie entfaltet, als während des Ersten Weltkriegs die europäischen Monarchien ins Wanken gerieten und Mitteleuropa nach 1918 von republikanischen und sozialrevolutionären Hoffnungen erfüllt war. Eine ganze Generation jüngerer Architekten in Berlin, Wien, Prag, Budapest und Moskau lebte im Fiebertraum von profanen Berufungsvisionen und religiösen Erweckungserlebnissen. Die Baumeister schwärmten von der Rückkehr des emanzipierten neuen Menschen in den Naturzustand ursprünglicher Sinnlichkeit und schufen phantasmagorische Höhlen und Baugebirge, Wolkenbügel und fliegende Städte als Gemeinschaftssymbole und Siegestempel der befreiten Völker.

Diesem gesellschaftsverändernden Furor lagen die geistigen Bildungsgesetze eines außergewöhnlichen Kunstwollens zugrunde, die Gottfried Benn noch im Schicksalsjahr 1933 mit einem erhitzten Begriffs-Stakkato zu umreißen versuchte: «Futurismus als Stil, auch Kubismus genannt, in Deutschland vorwiegend als Expressionismus bezeichnet, vielfältig in seiner empirischen Abwandlung, einheit-

in its basic inner attitude as a demolition of reality, as a reckless going-to-the-roots-of-things to the point where they can no longer be shifted into the psychological process in a usable and individually and sensually tainted, falsified, softened manner but are looking forward to the rare vocation by the creative spirit in the a-causal permanent silence of the absolute I."

In the field of fine arts, this radical demolition was equal to the Cubists' simultaneous perspectives of manifold perceptions of movement; in architecture, the most uncompromising response to the collective fantasies of origin and departure was the anti-individualistic art of the Supremacists and Constructivists, who wanted to break with the traditional direction of European art history through the pathos of a-causal self-explanation.

Zaha Hadid's intellectual relationship with the heroes of Russian revolutionary architecture of the twenties – Malevitch, Leonidov, El Lissitzky, Melnikov – is well known. Hadid, who was born in Baghdad in 1950, has set herself the task of bringing to fruition the interrupted experiments of new world designs. Her work loses nothing of the immediacy or explosiveness of the original efforts.

What El Lissitzky created with his space and body studies, the "Prouns", and Malevitch with his "architecton" models, was the expression of a yearning for departure and a belief in the future reflected in exciting new building

ideas and spatial visions. The Russian Constructivists created paintings and sculptures as preliminary architectural studies that tried to grasp artistically the revolution in technology since the turn of the century. Their drawings show imaginary moonscapes and planetary systems as vivid equivalents of experiences that evade sensory perception: electrical voltage, magnetic fields, radiant energy and movement.

Three quarters of a century later, this last great epoch of Modernism seems like a bygone future whose long-term consequences in the shape of industrial production, war economics and a destroyed ecology can be undone only with great difficulty. If one hopes to discover a new Constructivism with Zaha Hadid, it is one that has been cleansed by intellectual progress and to which Gottfried Benn's phrase of the absolute I and its creative vocation almost applies. It is the overcoming of the first Modernism through the demolition of progress, a repeated going-to-the-roots-of-things to get back beyond the point where the visions of the period between the wars degenerated into totalitarian and destructive ideologies.

Following her first work in Weil am Rhein, the Vitra Fire Station in 1993, Zaha Hadid then designed a visitors' pavilion that was commissioned by the city for the gardening show in 1999; it expands the architect's abstract radical Constructivism in a new way by making hereto-

und Zukunftsgläubigkeit, die sich in erregend neuen Bauideen und Raumvorstellungen niederschlug. Die russischen Konstruktivisten schufen Bilder und Plastiken als architektonische Vorstudien, die die technischen Umwälzungen seit der Jahrhundertwende künstlerisch zu fassen versuchten. Ihre Zeichnungen zeigen imaginäre Mondlandschaften und Planetensysteme als anschauliche Gegenwerte zu Erfahrungen, die sich der sinnlichen Wahrnehmung entzogen: elektrische Spannung, magnetische Kraftfelder, Strahlungsenergie und Bewegung.

Ein Dreivierteljahrhundert später erscheint diese letzte große Epoche der Moderne als vergangene Zukunft, deren Langzeitfolgen in Form von industrieller Verschleißproduktion, Kriegswirtschaft und einer zerstörten Ökologie nur schwer zu beheben sind. Wenn man bei Zaha Hadid einen neuen Konstruktivismus zu entdecken glaubt, so ist es ein durch allen intellektuellen Fortschritt gereinigter Konstruktivismus, auf den fast Gottfried Benns Wort vom absoluten Ich und seiner schöpferischen Berufung zutrifft. Es ist die Überwindung der ersten Moderne durch Fortschrittszertrümmerung, ein nochmaliges An-die-Wurzel-der-Dinge-Gehen, um wieder hinter jenen kritischen Punkt zu gelangen, an dem die Visionen der Zwischenkriegszeit zu totalitären und zerstörerischen Ideologien degenerierten.

Nach ihrem Erstlingswerk in Weil am Rhein, der Vitra Fire Station von 1993, hat Zaha Hadid jetzt im Auftrag der Stadt für die Landesgartenschau 1999 einen Besucherpavillon entworfen, der auf neue Weise den abstrakten Radikalkonstruktivismus der Ar-

fore unknown references to nature and landscape.

The thirty-hectare grounds of the gardening show, situated to the south of Weil, transform a formerly incoherent area on the outskirts and a gravel pit into large-scale thematic areas which, as a recreation area with an adjoining natural preserve, form a lasting and enduring park landscape. The master plan was designed by the landscape architects Krupp, Losert + Partners from Denzlingen.

Like an artificial geological formation, Zaha Hadid's visitors' pavilion emerges from the ground directly next to the former gravel pit. In the elevation, the zestfully curved building looks like the track switches of a railroad yard. One track divides into several paths which then separate from one another and finally begin to cross and tangle with one another. The first path leads past the south of the pavilion, the second one leads across the building as a rooftop promenade, and the third deviates to the north, laterally crossing through the house at half-height. The architectural composition not only comprises the building volume and interior but also uses the paths as a third space-creating element, which turns the accessible sculpture into a three-dimensional "promenade architecturale".

What is unusual considering Zaha Hadid's work up to now is the borrowing of naturalist ground formations and ground waves as archi-

chitektin um ungekannte Natur- und Landschaftsbezüge erweitert.

Das dreißig Hektar große Gartenschaugelände im Süden von Weil gliedert ein vormals disperses Stadtrandgebiet mitsamt einer Kiesgrube in großflächige Themenbereiche, die eine dauerhafte und nachhaltige Grünlandschaft zur Naherholung mit benachbartem Naturschutzgebiet bilden. Der Masterplan wurde von den Landschaftsarchitekten Krupp, Losert + Partner aus Denzlingen erstellt.

Unmittelbar neben die ehemalige Kiesgrube schiebt sich Zaha Hadids Besucherpavillon wie ein Stück künstlicher Geologie aus dem Boden. In der Aufsicht gleicht der schwungvoll gebogene Bau der Gleisharfe eines Eisenbahngeländes. Eine Spur teilt sich in mehrere Wege auf, die voneinander wegstreben und sich schließlich kreuzen und verschlingen. Der erste Weg führt südlich am Pavillon vorbei, ein zweiter führt als Promenade auf dem Dach über das Gebäude hinweg, und ein dritter schert nördlich aus, um das Haus auf halber Höhe seitlich zu durchqueren. Die architektonische Komposition besteht nicht nur aus Baumasse und Innenraum, sondern benutzt die Wegeführung als drittes raumbildendes Element, das die begehbare Skulptur zu einer dreidimensionalen «promenade architecturale» macht.

Ungewohnt in Zaha Hadids bisherigem Werk sind die naturalistischen Anleihen von Geländeformationen und Bodenwellen als bauplastische Orientierungspunkte. Mehr noch als an Eisenbahngleise läßt das Haus an Erdrutschformationen oder Geröll-Lawinen denken: Das von Westen aus sanft aufstei-

tectural-sculptural points of orientation. The house reminds one more of landslide formations or avalanches of rubble than of railroad tracks: the path bundle softly rising from the west rears above the main structure and abruptly ends in a shovel-like west front, which seems to push away the earth with an inclined haunch rounded towards the bottom. The tempo of the building's movement changes accordingly: at first, the roof sheet runs out above the café to the south, then, a little later, it follows the abruptly frozen gesture of the "earth shovel" at the north side, while the roof promenade in the center far exceeds the building's borders as a self-supporting bridge and only then leads back to the ground as wide outdoor steps.

Contrary to the crystal-clear abstraction of the entirely self-referential Fire Station, whose wall discs hold together in an ideal balance without any external influence, the gardening show pavilion rises from the ground like a chthonic creature whose direction of movement is linear through adaptation to the under-

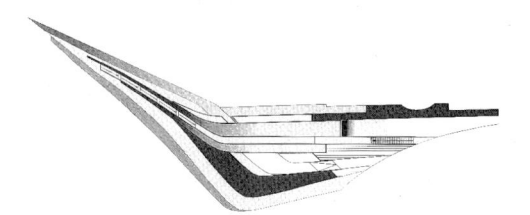

gende Wegebündel bäumt sich über dem Hauptbau auf und endet abrupt in einer schaufelartigen Westfront, die mit einer abwärts gerundeten Voute das Erdreich wegzuschieben scheint. Entsprechend verändern sich die Bewegungstempi des Gebäudes: Zuerst läuft die Dachbahn über dem Café im Süden aus, danach folgt wenig später die abrupt eingefrorene Geste der «Erdschaufel» an der Nordseite, während die Dachpromenade in der Mitte als freitragende Brücke noch weit über die Gebäudegrenze hinausläuft und erst danach als breite Freitreppe wieder auf den Erdboden zurückführt.

Im Gegensatz zur kristallklaren Abstraktion der völlig selbstreferentiellen Fire Station, deren Wandscheiben wie suprematistische Schwebebalken ohne äußere Einwirkungen in idealer Balance zusammenhalten, erhebt sich der Gartenschau-Pavillon wie ein chthonisches Urwesen aus dem Boden, dem die Anverwandlung an den Untergrund die lineare Bewegungsrichtung vorgibt. Die stromlinienförmigen Windungen des architektonischen Wegebündels sind strenggenommen keine raumbildenden, sondern raumaussparenden Elemente, zwischen denen sich die Nutzräume des Cafés, Ausstellungssaales und Umweltzentrums im buchstäblichen Sinne beiläufig entfalten.

Handelt es sich bei der Fire Station um eine eher additive Methode des Ineinander- und Übereinanderfügens selbständiger Wand- und Deckenscheiben, so besteht der Landesgartenschau-Pavillon aus der umbauten Leere der Wegebündel, die den nutzbaren Raum eher subtraktiv aus dem Volumen heraus-

ground. The streamlined bends of the architectural path bundle are, if seen strictly, not space-creating but rather space-avoiding elements in between which the ancillary rooms, the café, the exhibition hall and the environmental centre literally unfold in passing.

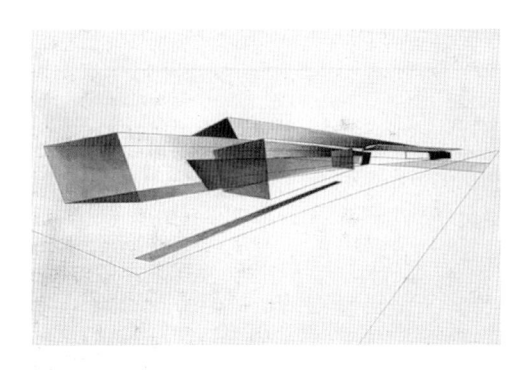

Whereas the Fire Station represents a rather additive method of joining together and layering independent wall and ceiling discs, the gardening show pavilion consists of the enclosed void of the path bundles which peel the usable space out of the volume in a reductive manner. The continuation of the roof promenade leads down to the ground floor in the two-story exhibition space via a serpentine ramp. Despite the horizontal grounds, the effect of the window strips, set off in their height at the closed north and opened south flank, results in diagonal lighting that creates the impression that the building is situated on a distinct hill.

schälen. Die Fortsetzung der Dachpromenade führt im doppelgeschossigen Ausstellungsraum über eine serpentinenförmige Rampe ins Erdgeschoß hinab. Trotz des waagerechten Geländes ergeben die höhenversetzten Fensterbänder an der geschlossenen Nord- und der geöffneten Südflanke eine Diagonalbelichtung, die den Eindruck erwecken, als befinde sich der Bau in einer ausgeprägten Hanglage.

Während die Fire Station durch das Gleichgewicht auseinanderstrebender und ineinander verkeilter Segmente einen idealen Gravitationspunkt andeutet, der sich zu völliger Schwerelosigkeit auszubalancieren scheint, vermag die Bodenschwere der topographisch motivierten Linearität des Gartenschau-Gebäudes solche Selbstaufhebungskräfte nicht zu entfalten. Der Pavillon hat in West-Ost-Richtung einen sanft definierten Anfang und ein kaskadenartiges Ende, so daß erst die Verbindung mit der Landschaft die Gebäudegrenzen aufhebt. Die kontinuierliche Wegeführung öffnet die Geschlossenheit des Pavillons auf die Umgebung hin, wodurch keine definitive Grenze, sondern ein steter Raumfluß von außen nach innen entsteht.

Auf ähnliche Weise einen Raumfluß zwischen Bauwerk und Umgebung hatte Zaha Hadid 1994 mit dem noch unrealisierten Projekt «Spittelau» in Wien geschaffen. Es ging ebenfalls um die Revitalisierung eines ehemaligen Industriegeländes auf einem Uferstreifen am Donaukanal, der von einer bestehenden Eisenbahnbrücke des Wiener Architekten Otto Wagner durchschnitten wird. Weil die funktionslose Brükke erhalten werden sollte, plante Zaha Hadid eine Art

While the Fire Station hints at an ideal point of gravitation through a balance between dispersing and interconnected segments which seems to balance out into an overall weightlessness, the grounded mass of the topographically motivated linearity of the gardening show building is incapable of unfolding such forces of self-cancellation. On the east-west axis, the pavilion has a softly defined beginning and a cascading end so that only the connection with the landscape terminates the borders of the building. The continuous paths open up the enclosure of the pavilion towards the environment, which creates not a definitive border but a constant spatial flow from outside to inside.

In 1994 Zaha Hadid created a spatial flow between building and environment in a similar way with the unrealized project "Spittelau" in Vienna. The issue was also the revitalization of a former industrial area on a strip of land along the banks of the Danube canal through which an existing railroad bridge by the Viennese architect Otto Wagner passes. Since the bridge, which was without function, was to be preserved, Hadid planned a kind of modern "Ponte Vecchio", an inhabitable bridge. Similar to the "negative" path bundle in Weil am Rhein, a "positive" row of studios, apartments and offices meanders beneath, through and across the old railroad bridge like a volumetric ribbon. Cafés, shops and restaurants on the first floor of the building volume create the connection

moderne «Ponte Vecchio», eine bewohnbare Brücke. Ähnlich dem «negativen» Wegebündel in Weil am Rhein schlingt sich hier eine «positive» Reihe von Studios, Wohnungen und Büros wie ein volumetrisches Band unter, durch und über die alte Eisenbahnbrücke hindurch und hinüber. Cafés, Geschäfte und Restaurants im Erdgeschoß der Baukörper stellen die Verbindung zur Fußgängerpromenade am Flußufer her. Es handelt sich um eine parasitäre Anfügung eines neuen Objekts an den Bestand, einen Schmarotzer-Bau, der stark genug ist, selber zum Wirtskörper zu werden.

Auch der Gartenschau-Pavillon ist weniger der Gattung «Haus» als dem Bautypus «Brücke» zuzurechnen. 1996 hatte Zaha Hadid einen verwandten Entwurf für eine bewohnbare Brücke über die Londoner Themse vorgelegt, bei der die Funktion der Zirkulation und Verkehrserschließung erweitert und

with the pedestrian promenade along the river bank. It is a parasitic addition of a new object to the existing structure, a dependent building which is also strong enough in itself to become the host volume.

The gardening show pavilion, too, is less a part of the "house" species than it is a member of the "bridge" building type. In 1996, Zaha Hadid submitted a related design for an inhabitable bridge across the Thames River, in London; its function of circulation and traffic accessibility was extended and upvalued into usable spaces. Hadid's attempt to achieve the highest possible transparency with untreated, fair-faced concrete not only uses the physical movement energies of folded or opened-up volumes but also the alignment of the paths themselves.

She thus moves from the architectural metaphor of frozen movement to a structural analogy, which brings function and form into a higher balance. This third level can also be called "program." Program means an activist understanding of use that doesn't just determine the building's shape but is also generated by the building itself. These can be the platonically ideal empty spaces of a Mies van der Rohe but can also include the movement vectors and lines of force made visible by Hadid. By creating continuous volumes from lines and surfaces and by putting them into relation in a versatile way without any restriction placed on the per-

zu nutzbaren Räumen aufgewertet wurde. Zaha Hadids Versuch, mit unbehandeltem Sichtbeton größtmögliche Transparenz zu erreichen, nutzt nicht allein die physikalischen Bewegungsenergien gefalteter oder aufgebrochener Volumina, sondern die Gerichtetheit der Wegeführung selber.

Von der architektonischen Metapher der gefrorenen Bewegung geht sie damit zu einer Strukturanalogie über, die Funktion und Form in ein höheres Gleichgewicht bringt. Man kann diese dritte Ebene auch als «Programm» bezeichnen. Programm meint eine aktivische Auffassung von Nutzung, die nicht nur die Gebäudeform bestimmt, sondern auch selber vom Gebäude generiert wird. Das können die platonisch idealen Leerräume eines Mies van der Rohe sein, aber auch die sichtbar gemachten Bewegungssektoren und Kraftlinien von Zaha Hadid. Indem sie aus Linien und Flächen kontinuierliche Volumina erzeugt und diese – wie einst die Konstruktivisten und Kubofuturisten – ohne jede perspektivische Einzwängung und Verflachung möglichst vieldimensional in Beziehung setzt, schafft sie Gebäude, die keine fertigen Gebrauchsgegenstände abgeben, sondern vielmehr Drehbüchern voller dramatischer Raumszenen gleichen. Das Wichtigste ist nicht der verzerrte Baukörper, sondern die Leere und Offenheit zwischen den Fragmenten. Der Raum, das schlechthin Unsichtbare und Ungreifbare, ist der wahre Luxus, in dem Zaha Hadid schwelgt. Wo andere Architekten sich teure Materialschlachten liefern und einander mit aufwendigem Dekor überbieten, sucht sie den Raumluxus der reinen Leere.

spective and without any flattening – like the Constructivists and Cubist-Futurists used to do – she creates buildings that are not ready-made objects of daily use but rather resemble scripts full of dramatic spatial scenes. What is most important is not the distorted building volume but the void and openness between the fragments. Space, the simply invisible and intangible, is the true luxury in which Zaha Hadid revels. Where other architects fight expensive material battles and outdo one another with extravagant decor, she seeks for the spatial luxury of the pure void.

If Robert Musil's words that great architecture can be created only out of ideas of glorification apply, then Zaha Hadid's buildings are very special praises: the incorruptibility of the perfect architectural fantasy, transformability of large sunken utopias of Modernism into the present, self-reflection about the intellectual challenges of today's architecture and sensual certainty about the mathematical, geometrical bases of free spatial creations. Beauty is but a different word for it.

Michael Mönninger
Architectural critic, Berlin

Wenn Robert Musils Wort zutrifft, daß große Architektur nur aus Veherrlichungsgedanken entstehen kann, dann bilden Zaha Hadids Bauwerke ganz besondere Lobpreisungen: der Unbestechlichkeit der exakten architektonischen Phantasie, der Transformierbarkeit versunkener großer Moderne-Utopien in die Gegenwart, der Selbstreflexion über die intellektuellen Herausforderungen heutiger Baukunst und der sinnlichen Gewißheit über die mathematisch-geometrischen Grundlagen freier Raumschöpfungen. Schönheit ist dafür nur ein anderes Wort.

Michael Mönninger
Architekturkritiker, Berlin

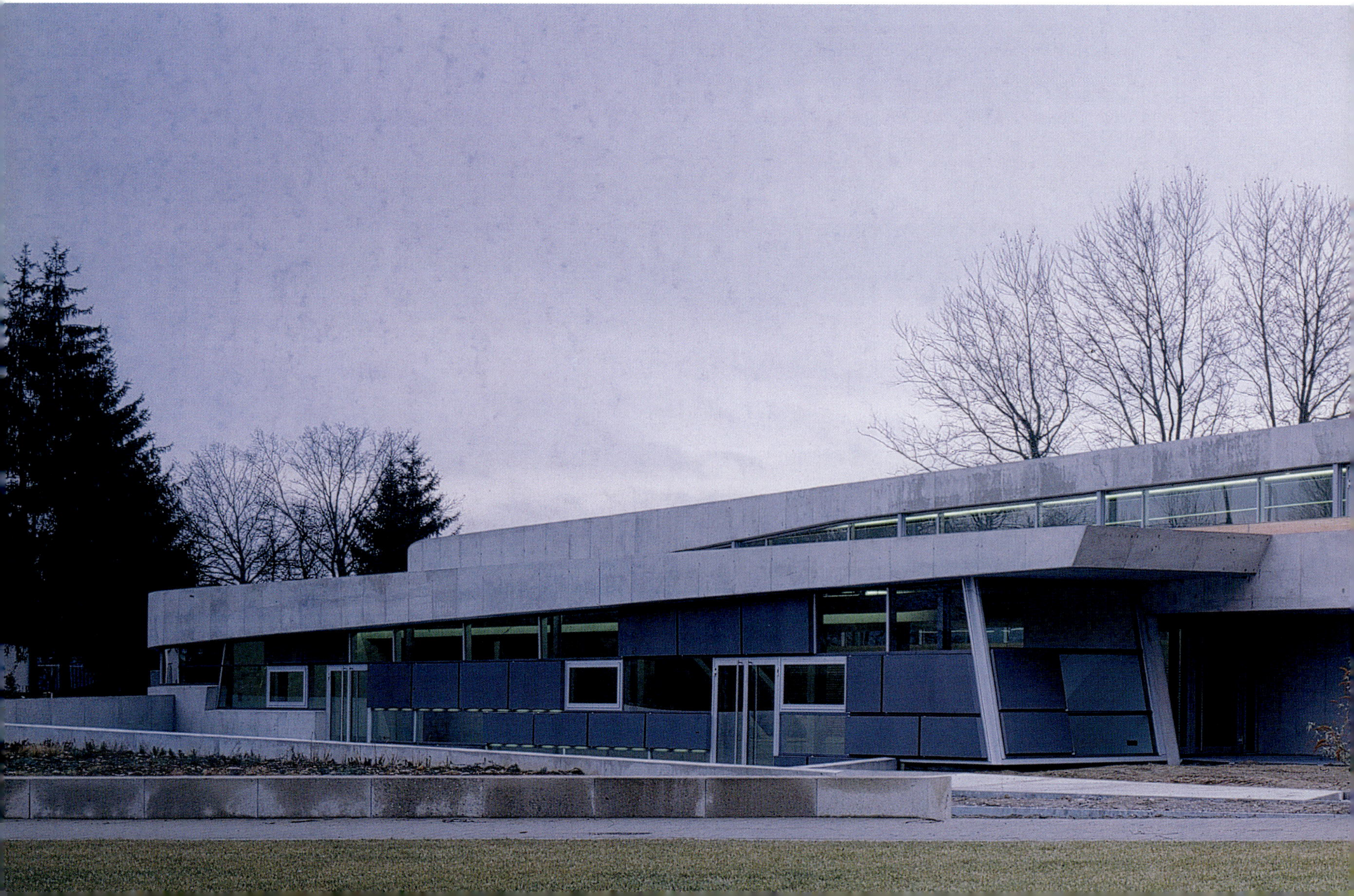

Promenade architecturale

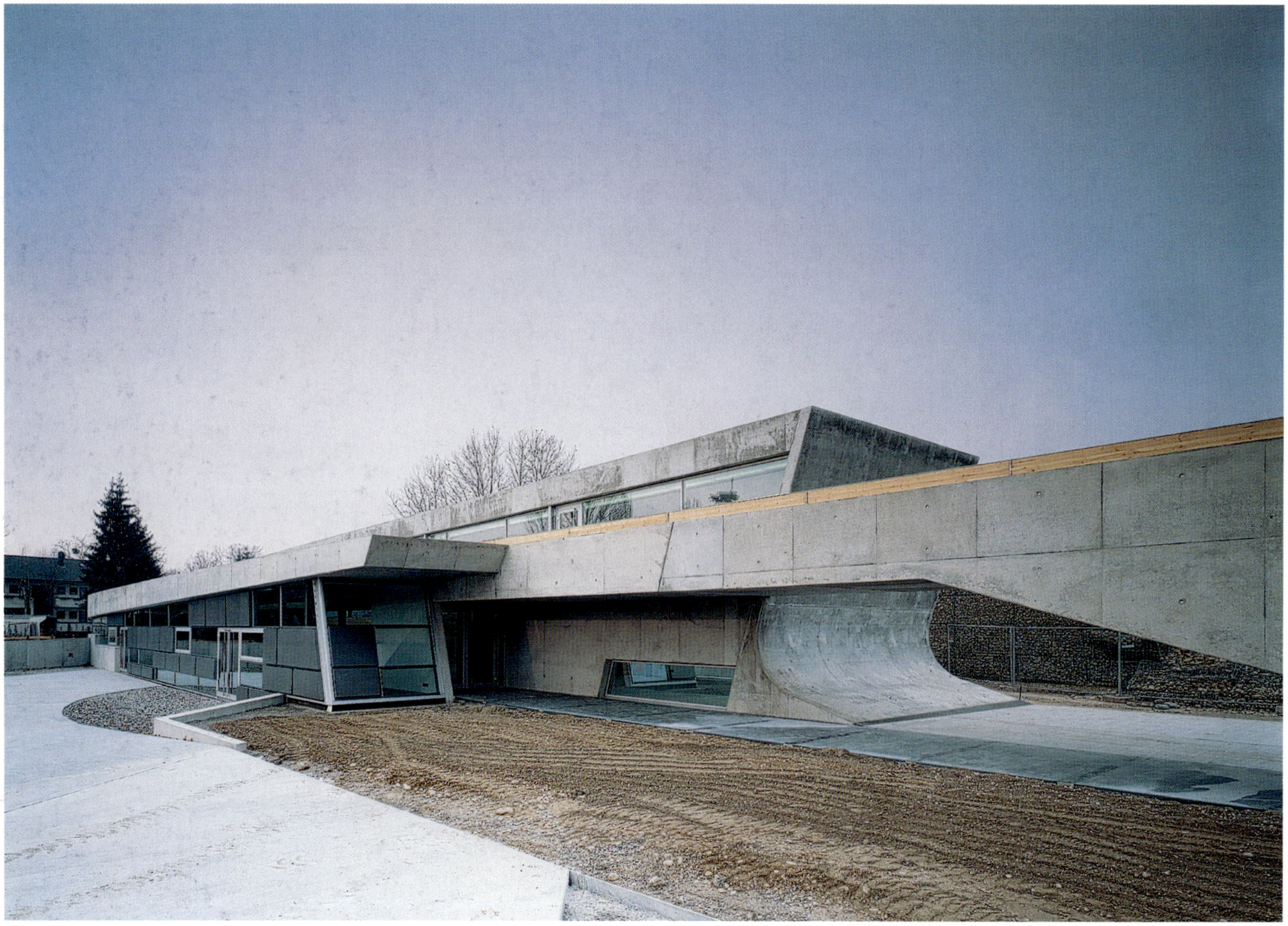

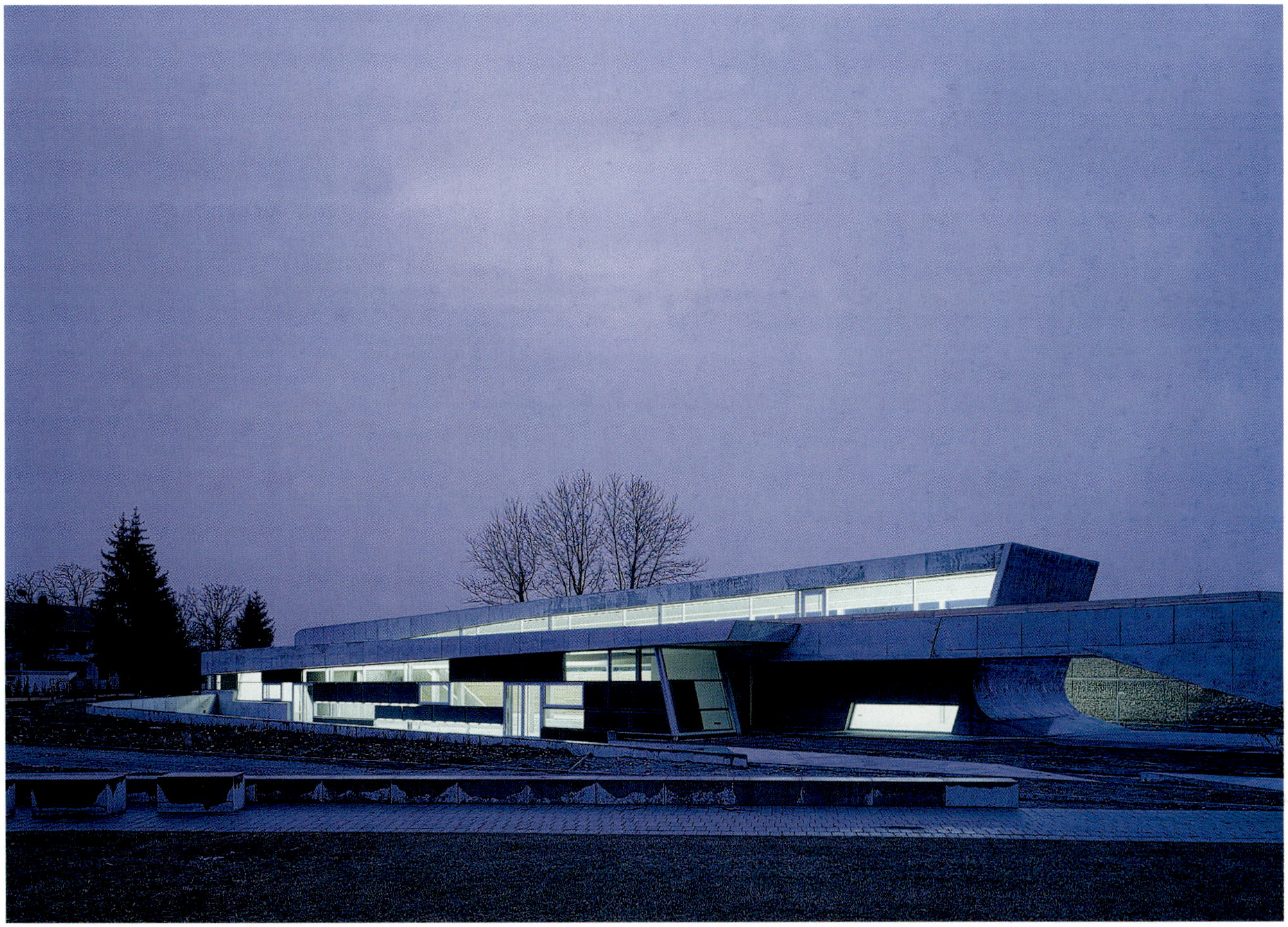

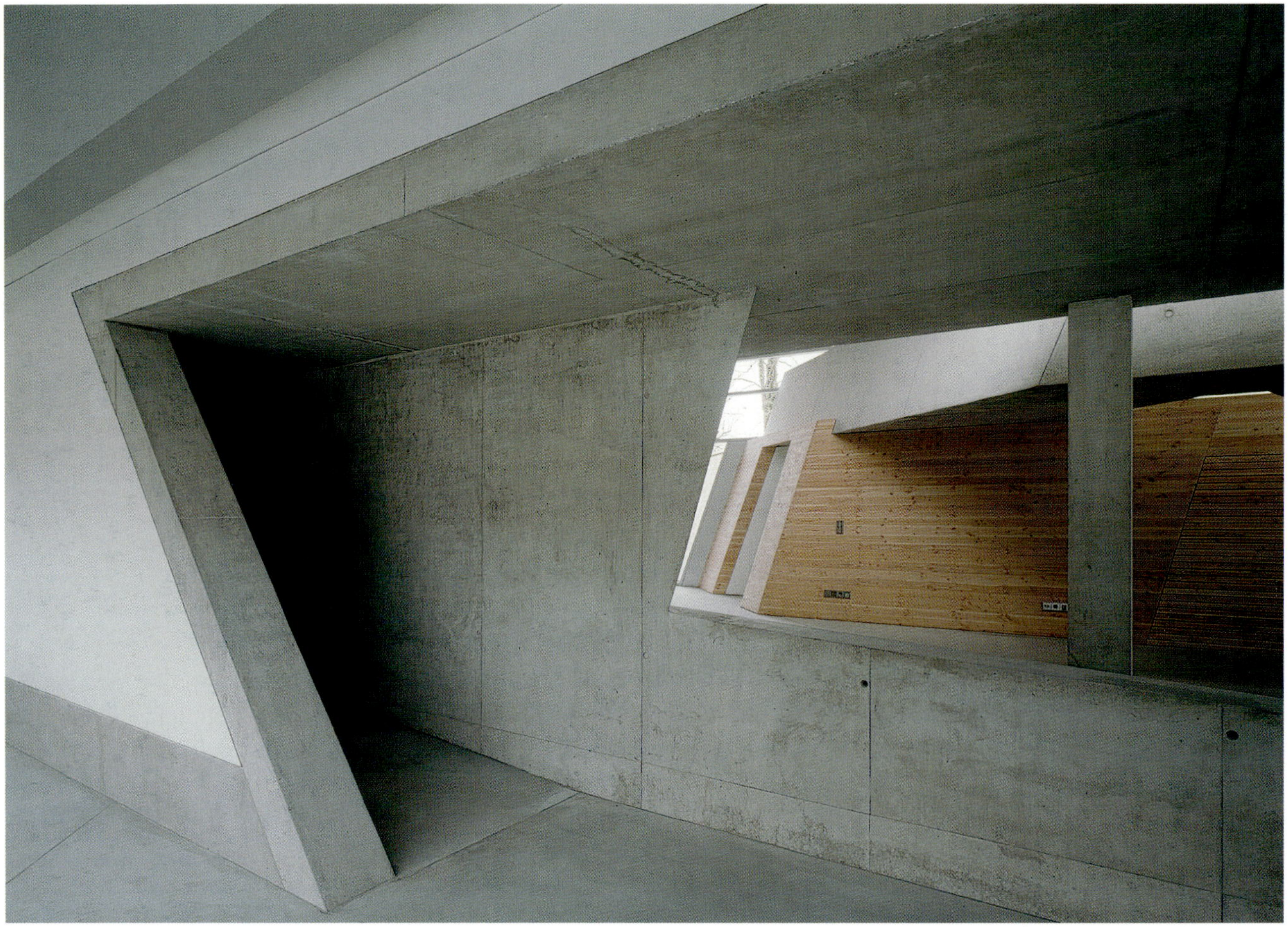

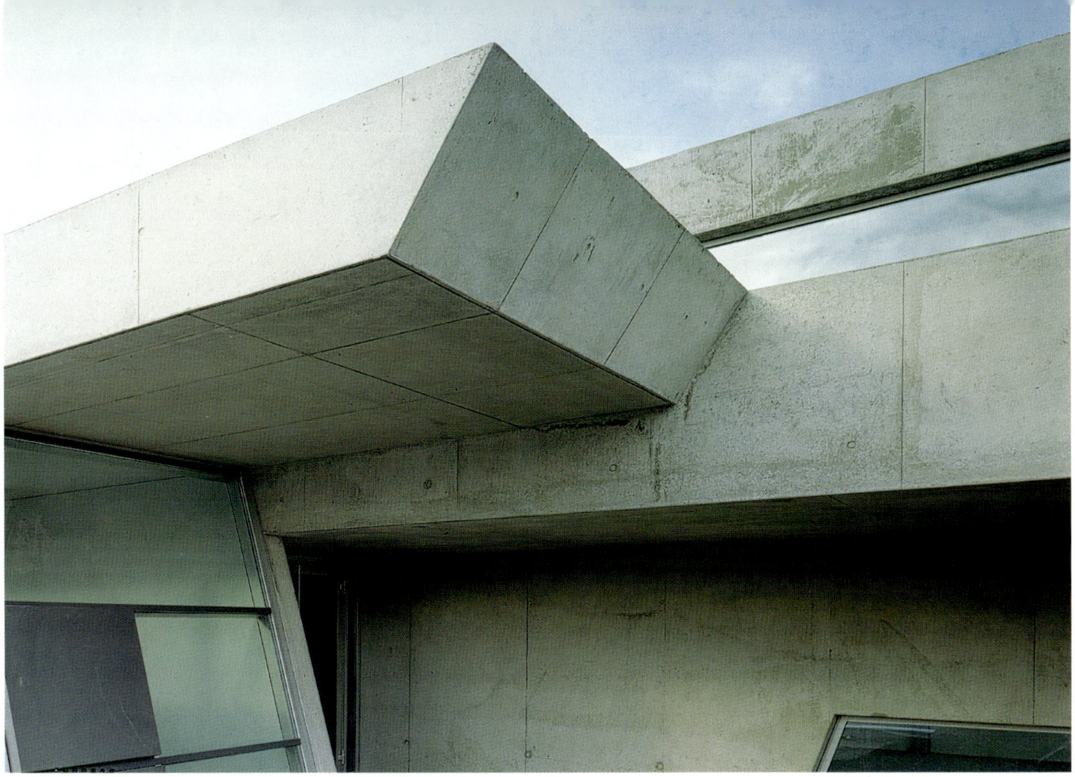

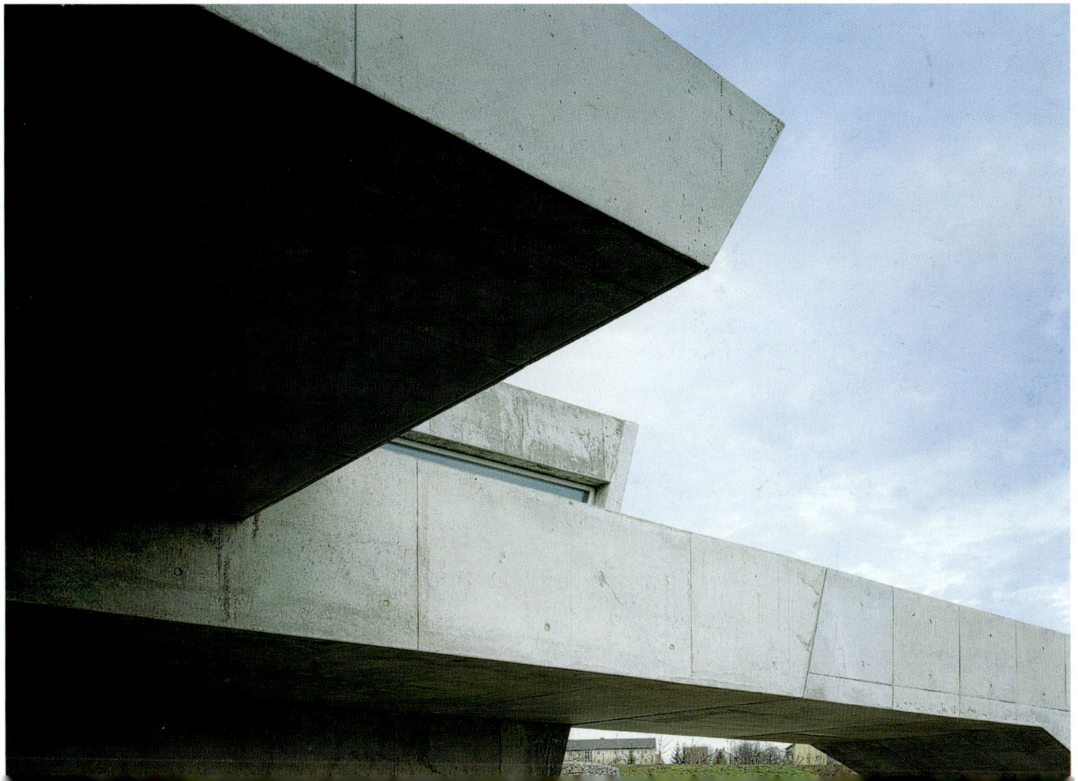

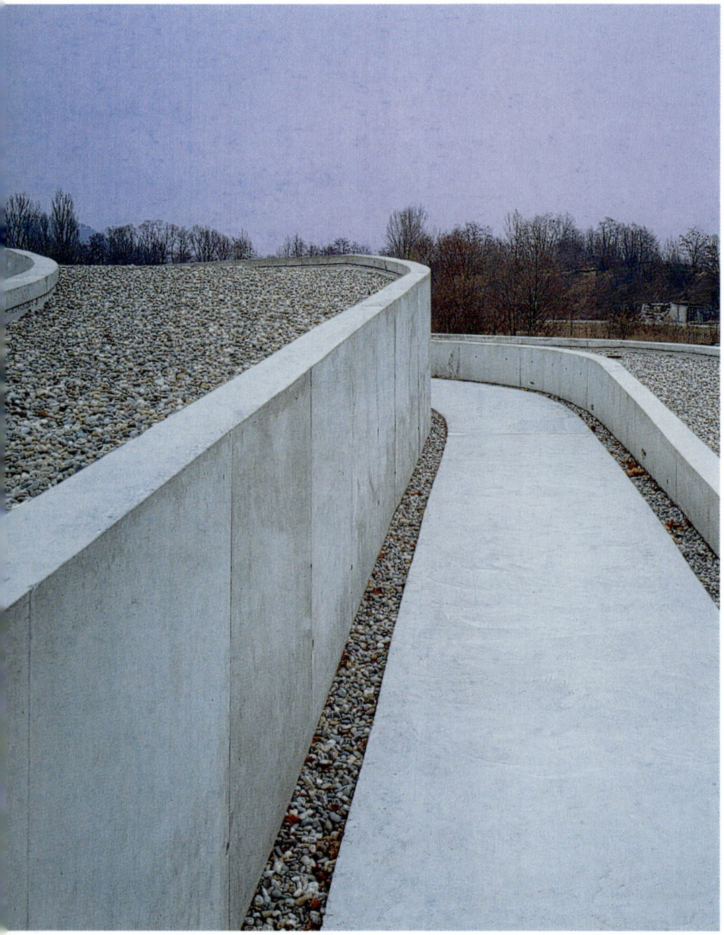

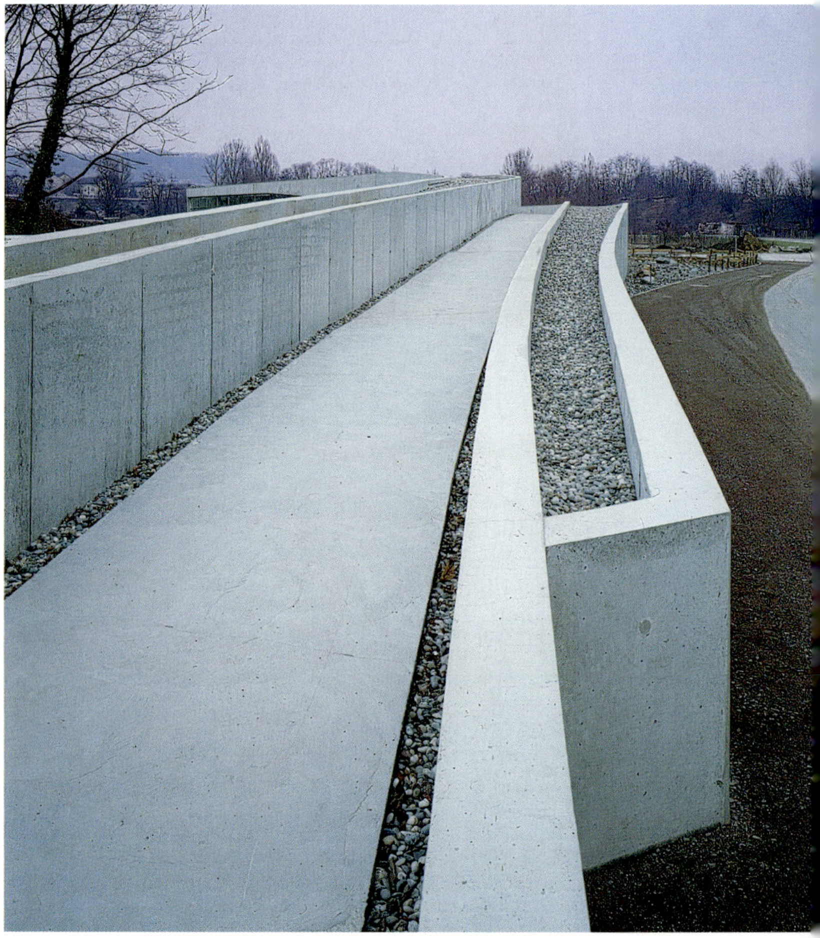

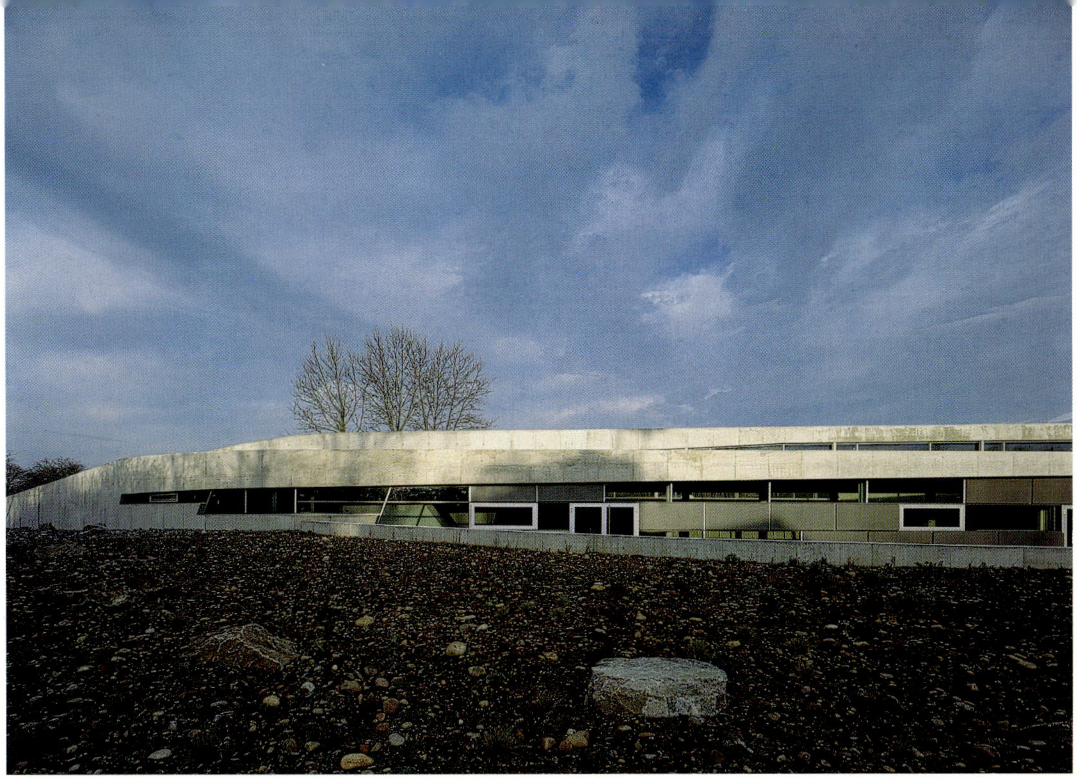

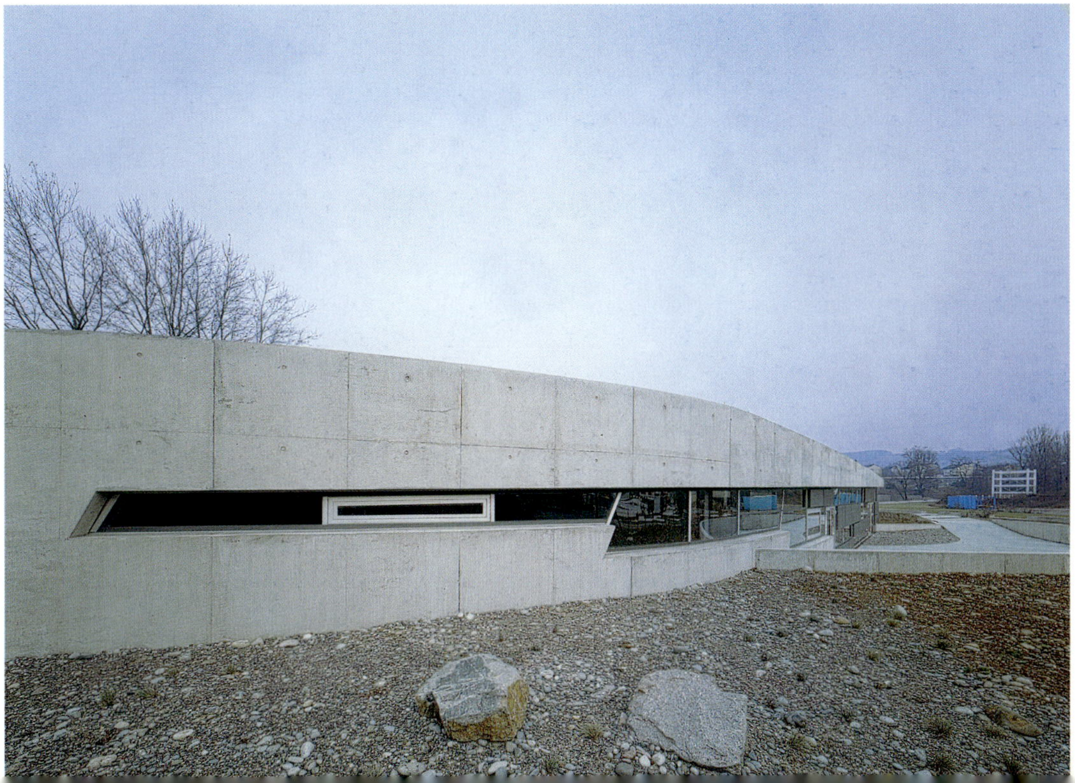

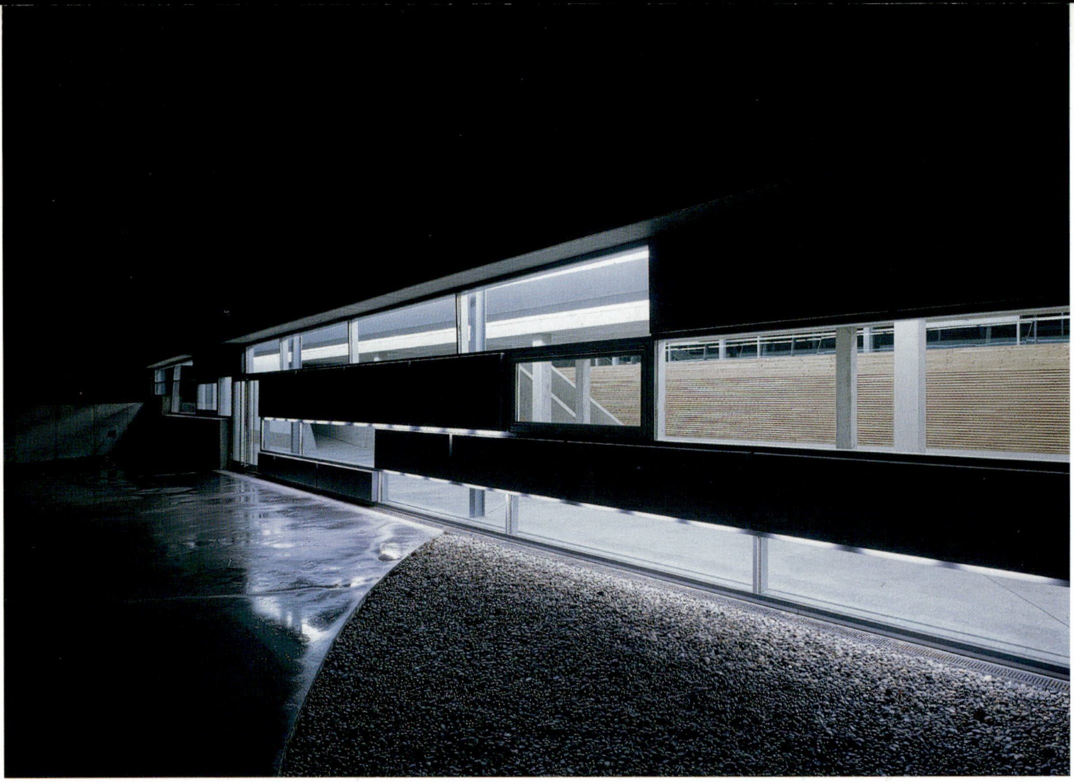

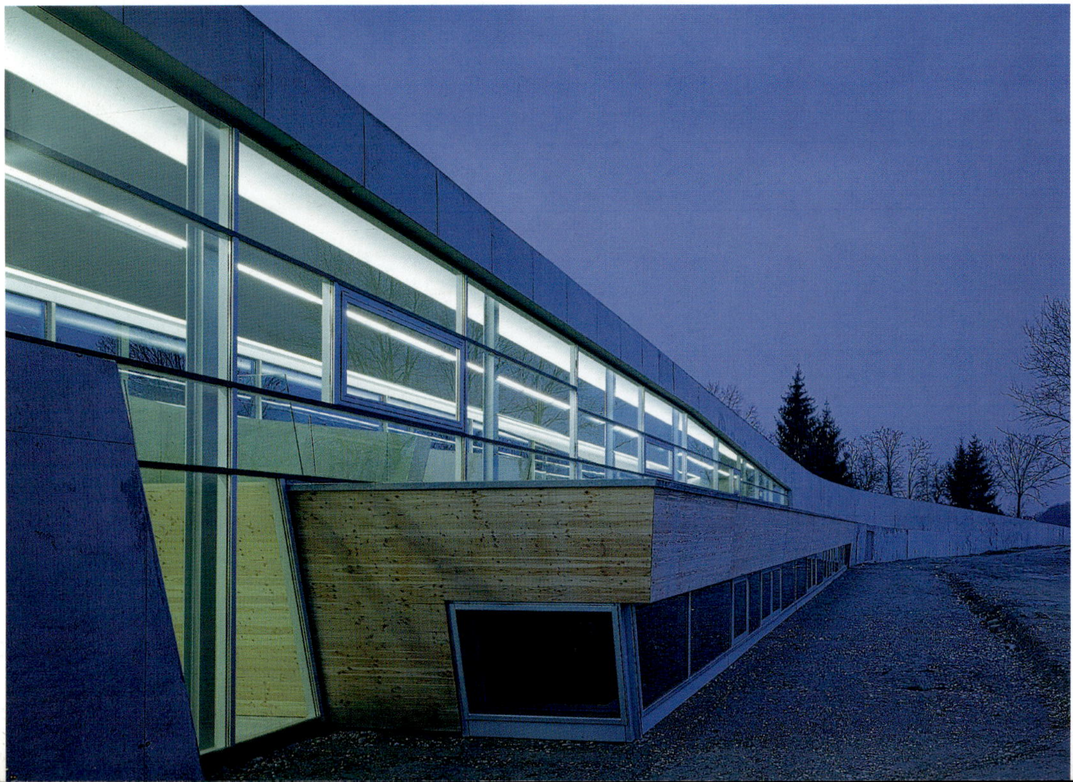

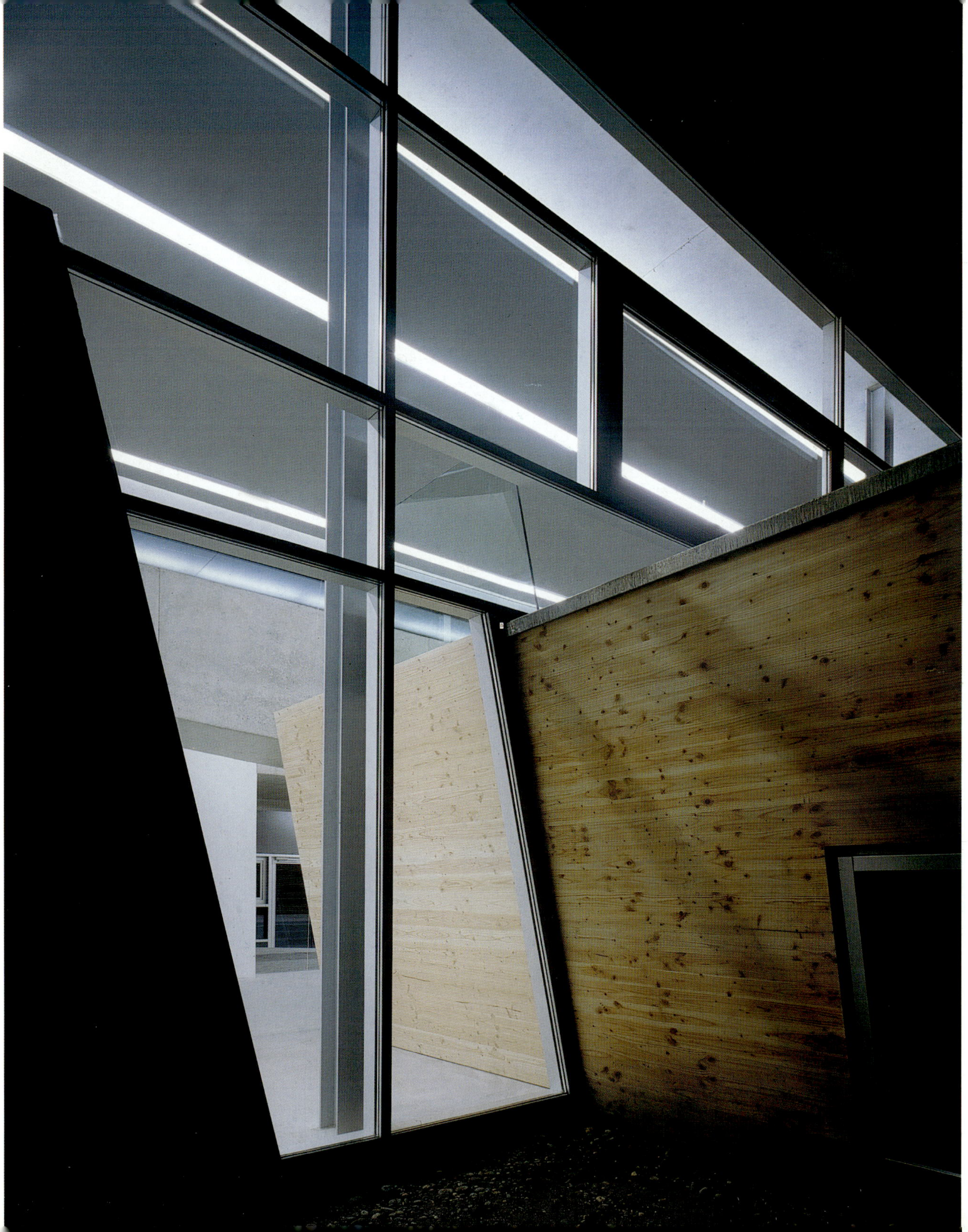

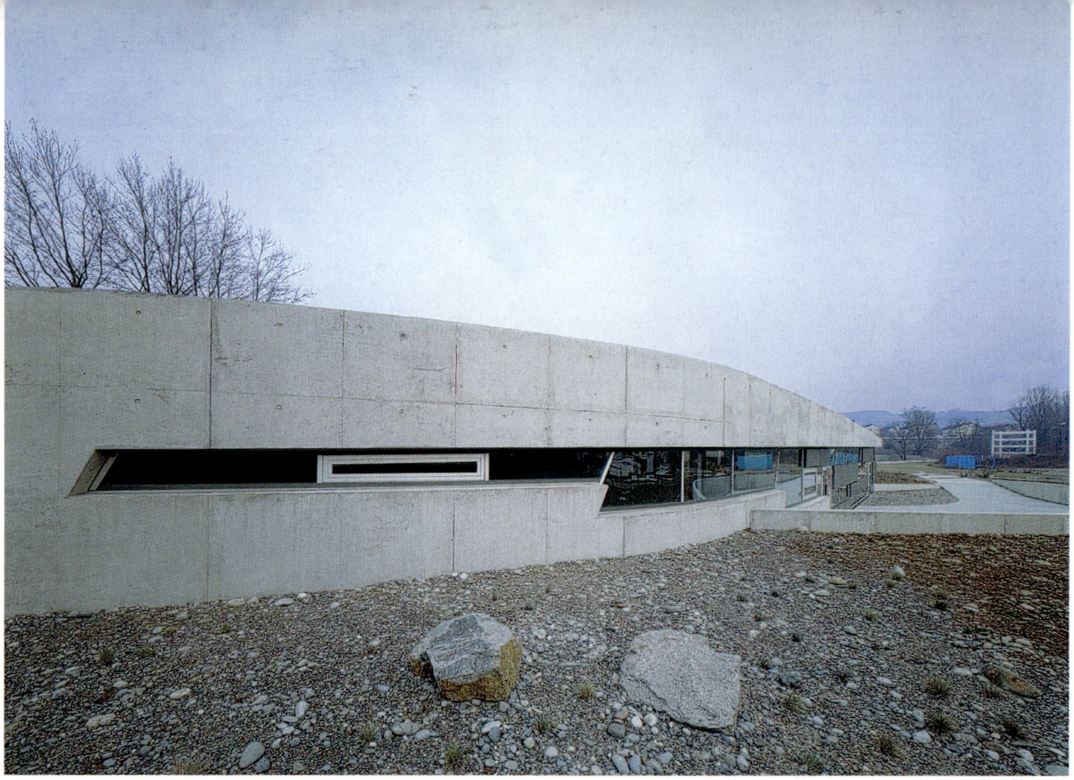

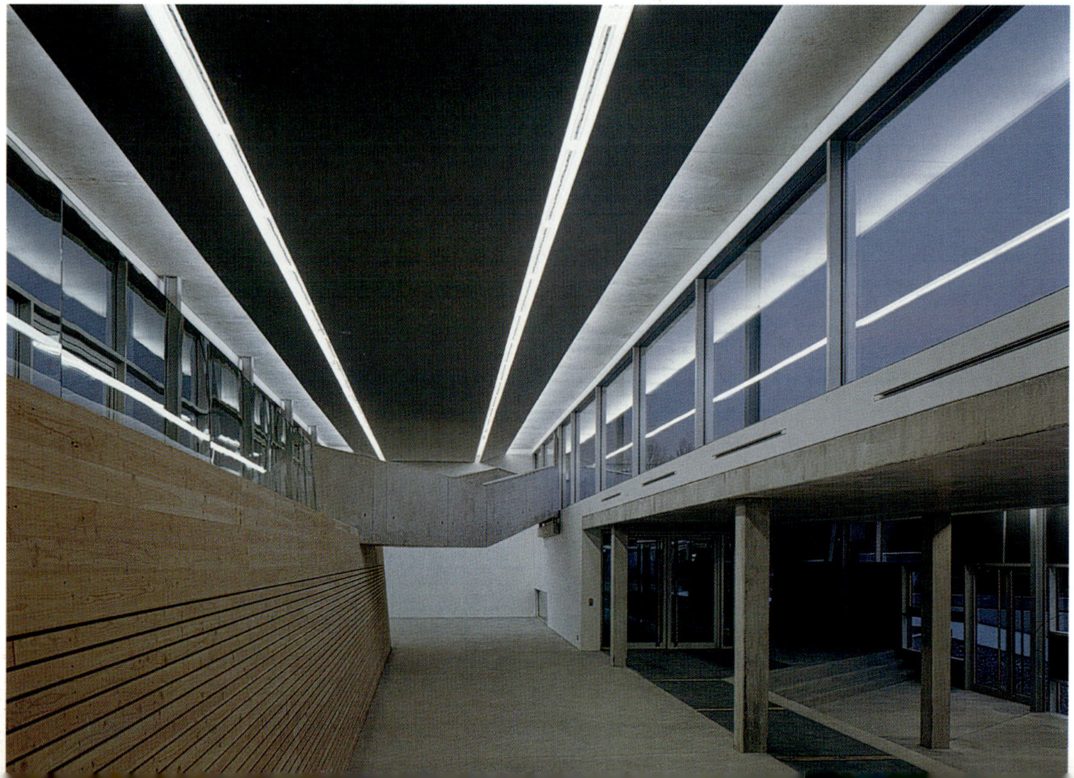

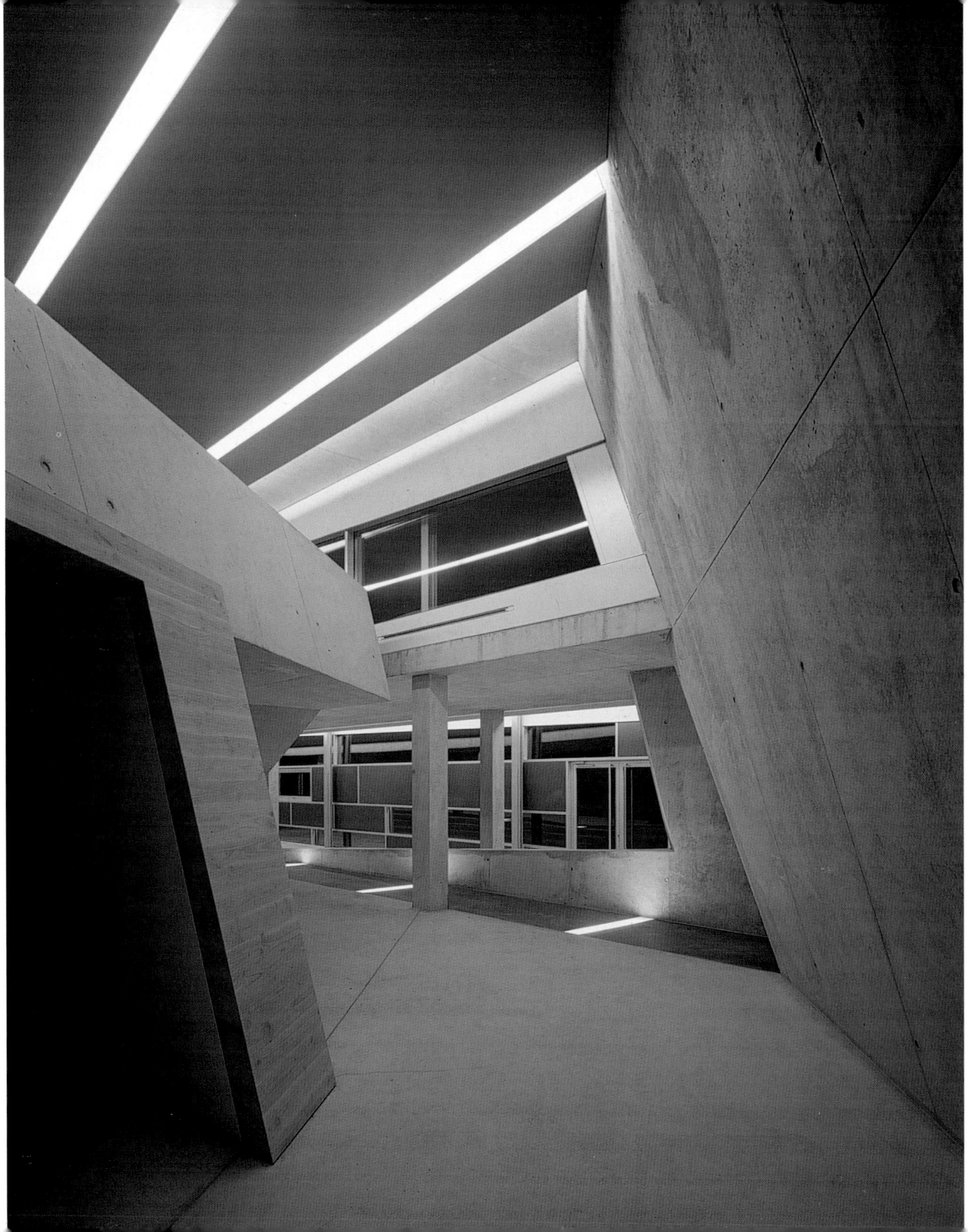

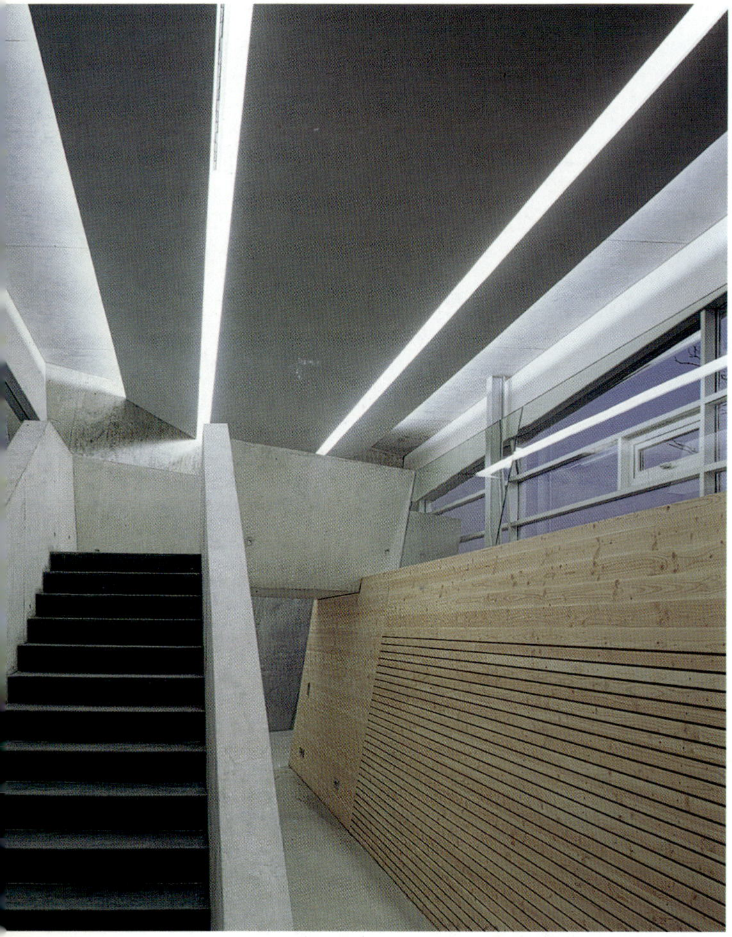

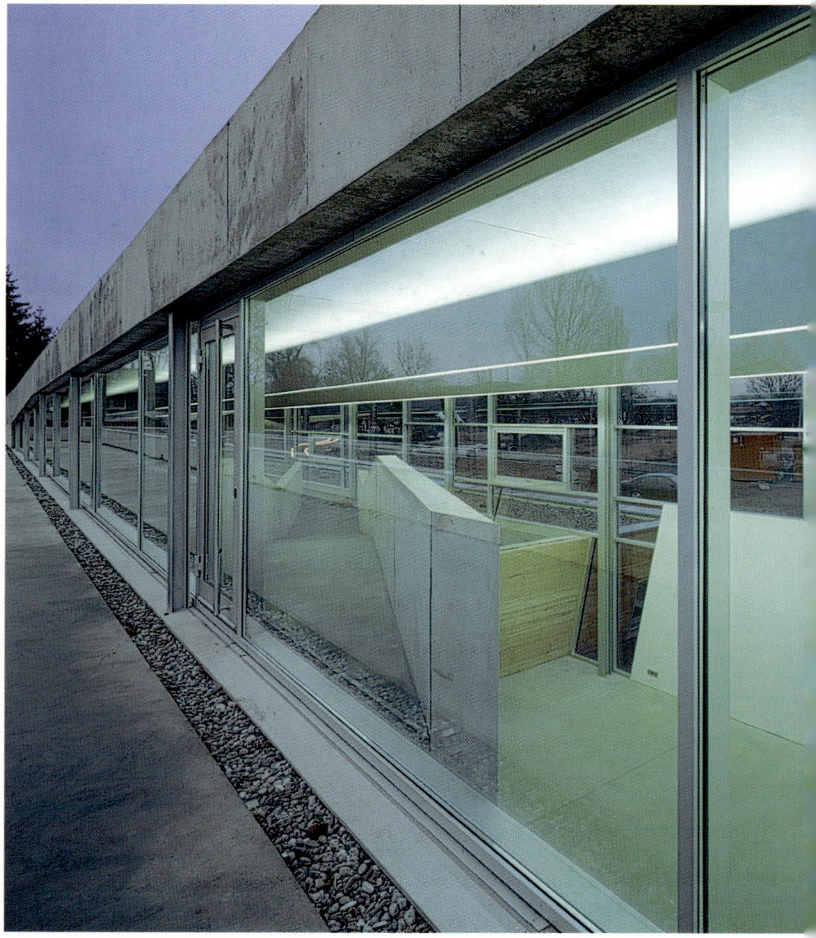

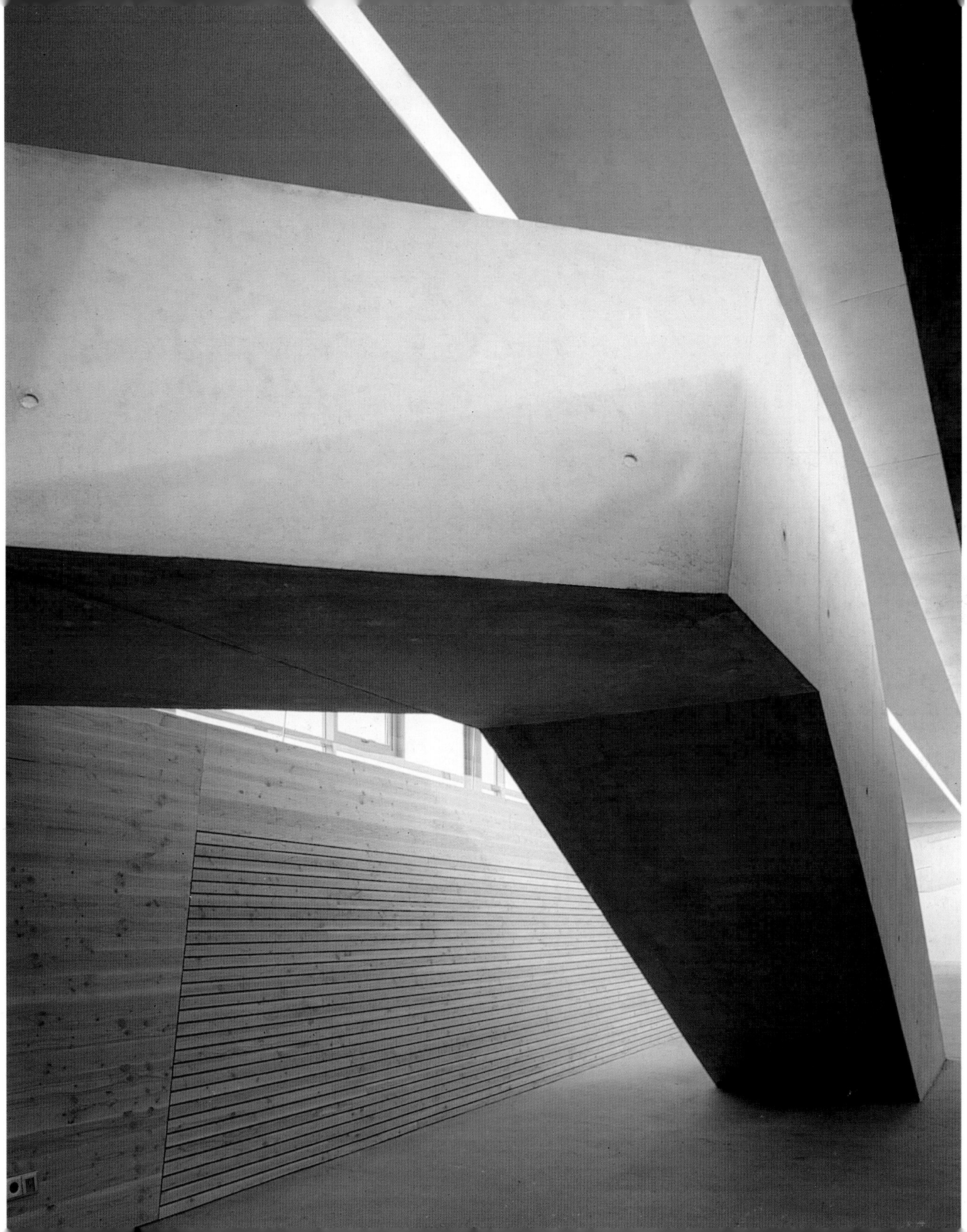

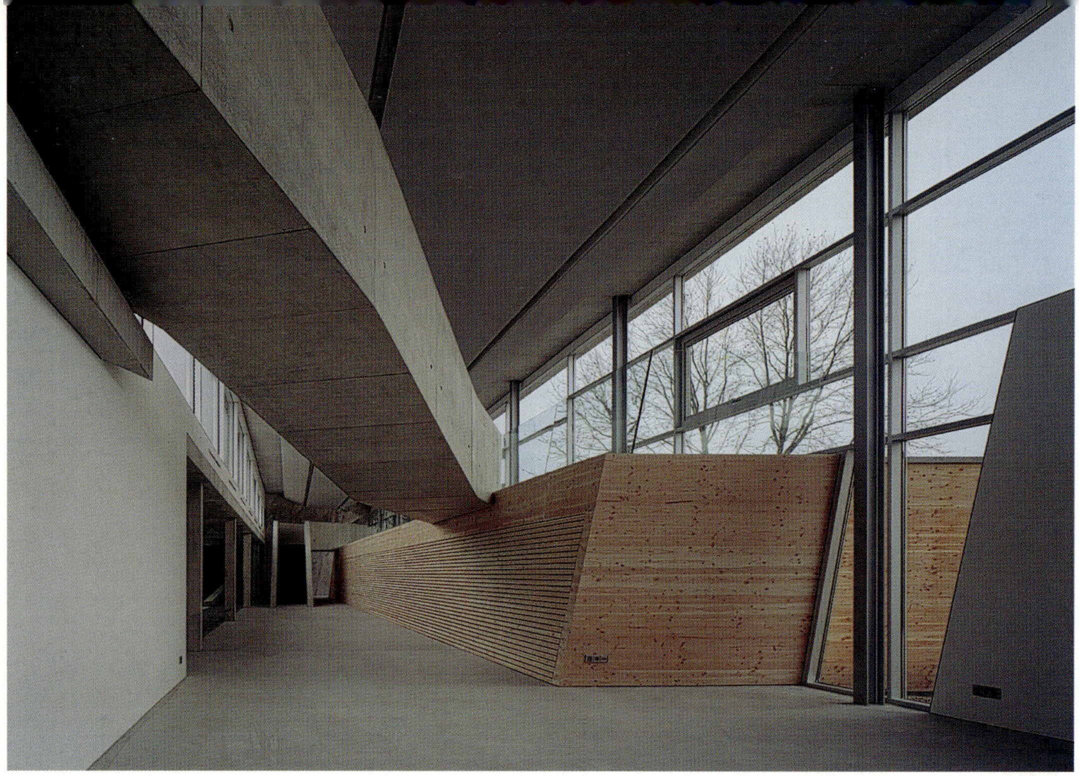

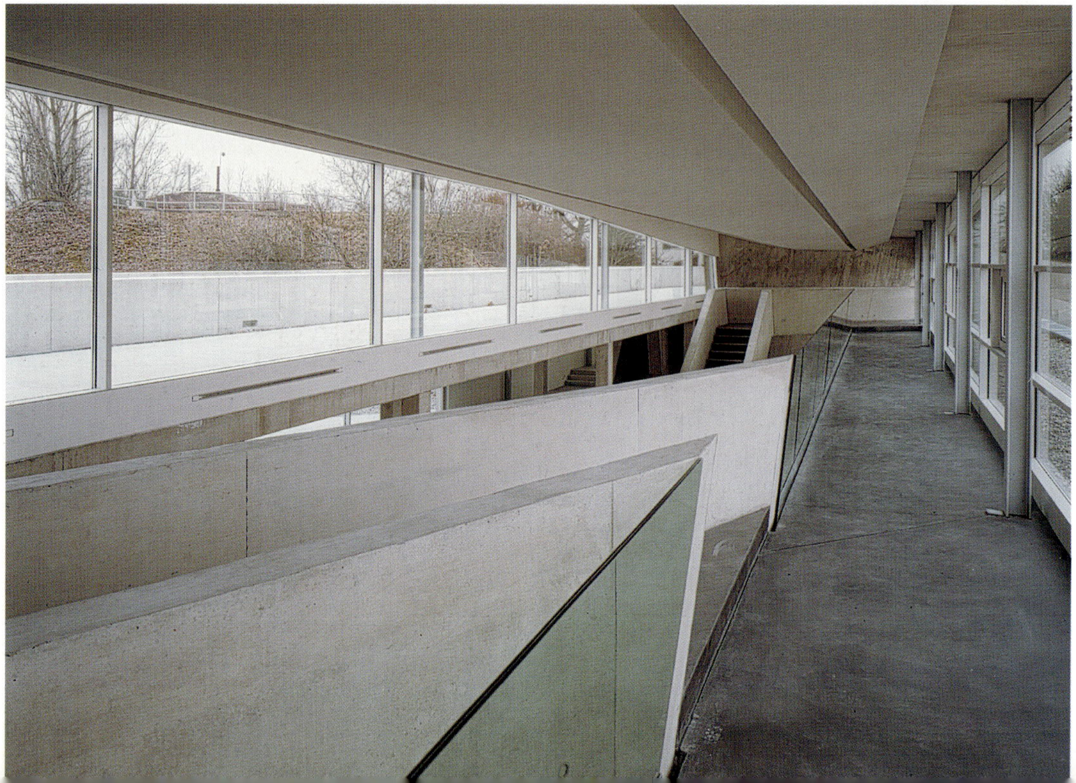

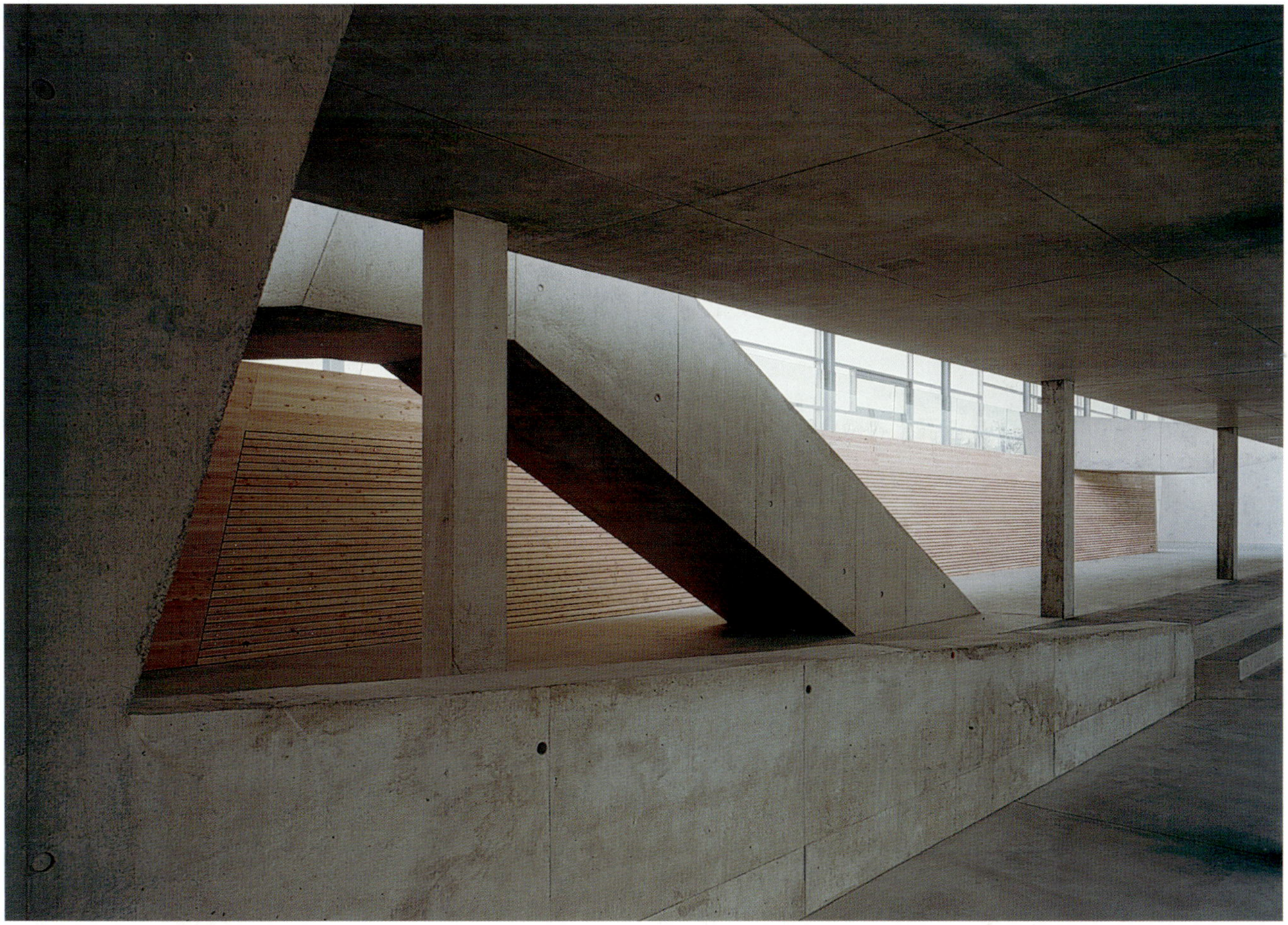

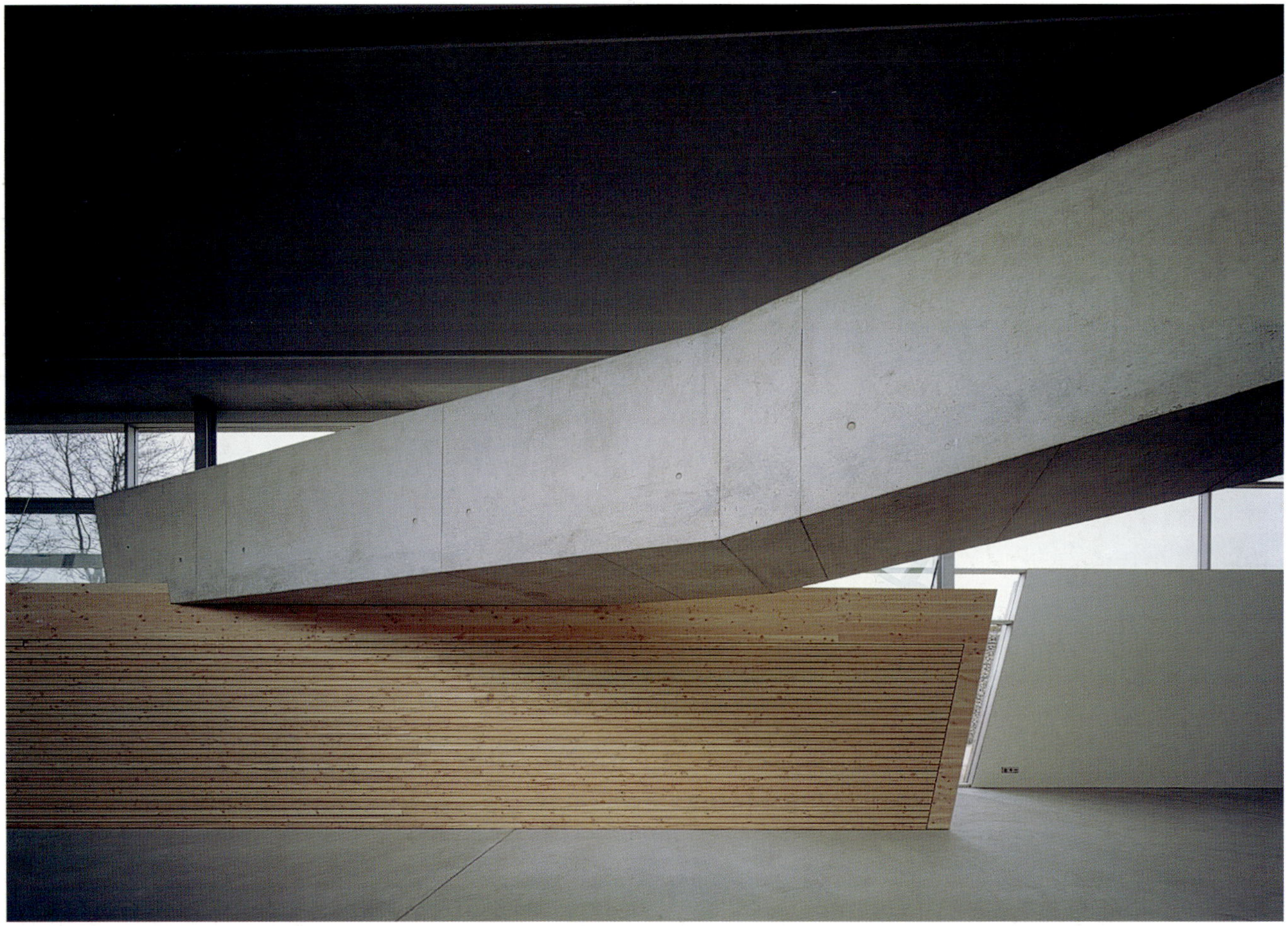

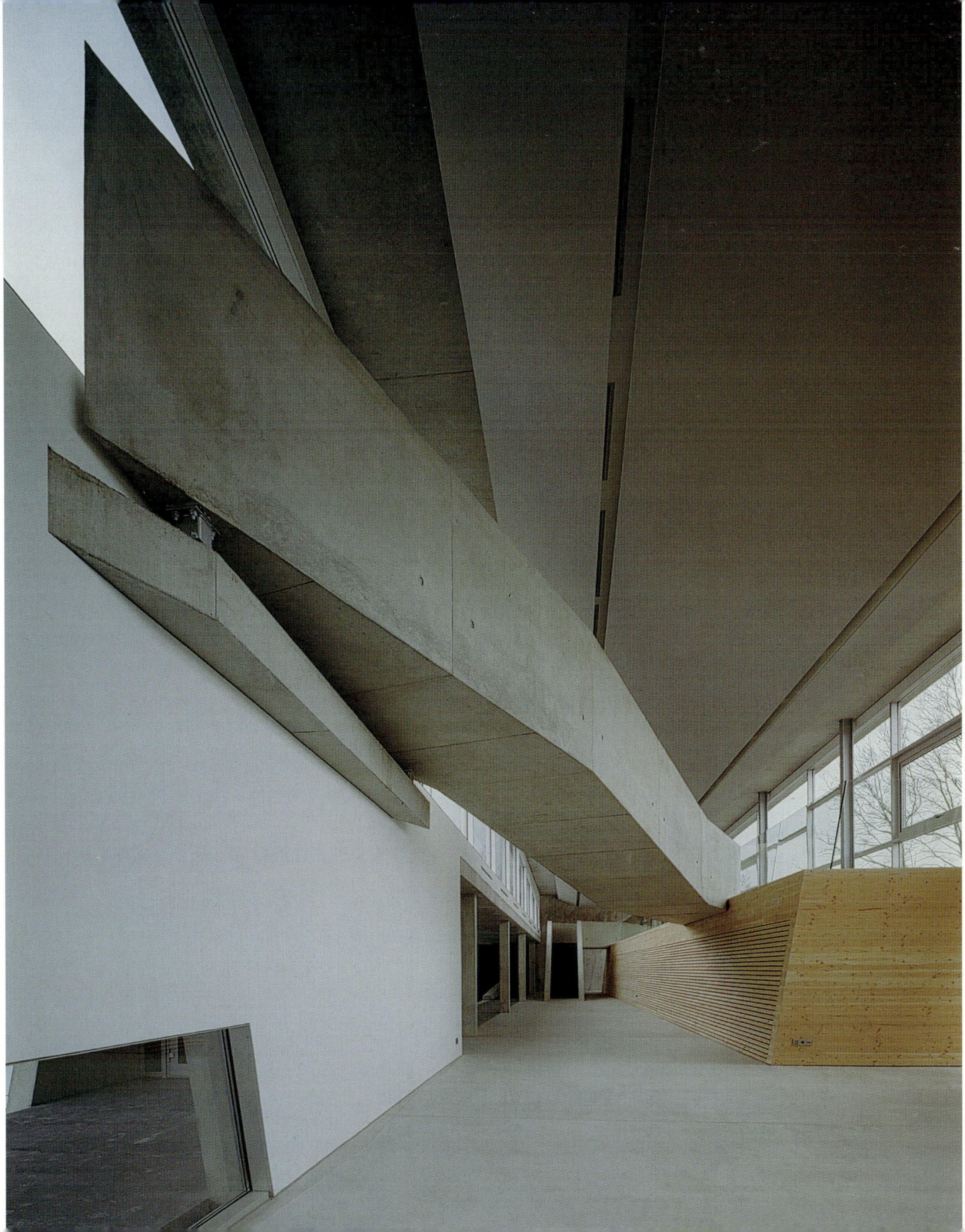

Biographies

Zaha Hadid, born in Baghdad, Iraq in 1950, began her study of architecture in 1972 at the Architectural Association in London and was awarded the Diploma Prize in 1977. She then joined the Office of Metropolitan Architecture, began teaching at the Architectural Association with Rem Koolhaas and Elia Zenghelis and later led her own studio at the AA until 1987. Her winning entry of The Peak Club, Hong Kong, in 1983 was followed by first place awards in competitions in Berlin, Düsseldorf, Cardiff and London. Completed projects include the Vitra Fire Station in Weil am Rhein, the installation for the exhibition The Great Utopia at the Solomon R. Guggenheim Museum in New York 1992 and other schemes in Berlin, Groningen and Sapporo.

At present Zaha Hadid works on a commission for the Contemporary Arts Center in Cincinnati, Ohio, the pavilion of the "Mind Zone" for the Greenwich Millenium Dome, and the Centre for Contemporary Arts in Rome.

Patrik Schumacher, born 1961 in Bonn.
Studied architecture at Stuttgart University. Since 1998 collaborator and since 1995 co-author and partner of several projects in the office Zaha M. Hadid.

Biographien

Zaha Hadid, geboren 1950 in Bagdad, Irak, begann ihr Architekturstudium 1972 an der Architectural Association in London und schloß es 1977 mit Diplom ab. Sie arbeitete danach im Stadtbauamt, unterrichtete an der Architectural Association gemeinsam mit Rem Koolhaas und Elia Zenghelis, und leitete bis zum Jahr 1987 ihr eigenes Atelier in der AA. Ihrer preisgekrönten Eingabe zum Peak Club, Hong Kong, 1983 folgten erste Plätze bei Wettbewerben in Berlin, Düsseldorf, Cardiff und London. Realisierte Projekte sind, u.a., das Vitra Feuerwehrgerätehaus in Weil am Rhein, die Installation für die Ausstellung The Great Utopia im Solomon Guggenheim Museum New York 1992 sowie weitere Projekte in Berlin, Groningen und Sapporo.

Zur Zeit arbeitet Zaha Hadid an einem Auftrag für das Contemporary Arts Center in Cincinnati, Ohio, dem Pavillon der «Mind Zone» für den Greenwich Millenium Dome, sowie dem Centre for Contemporary Arts in Rom.

Patrik Schumacher, geboren 1961 in Bonn.
Architekturstudium an der Universität Stuttgart. Seit 1988 Mitarbeit und seit 1995 Mitautor und Partner an mehreren Projekten im Büro Zaha M. Hadid.

Seit 1995 Direktor des Graduate Design Programmes «Design Research Laboratory» an der Architectural Association, London.

Since 1995 director of the Graduate Design Program "Design Research Laboratory" at the Architectural Association, London.
1994–1998 guest professorships: Harvard University, University of Illinois at Chicago, Columbia University, N.Y.

roland mayer, born 1956 in altötting/bavaria.
after training as an architectural draftsman, he studied architecture. in partnership with günther pfeifer, realization of building projects with zaha hadid, frank o. gehry, tadao ando and alvaro siza in weil am rhein, with frank o. gehry in basel (ch).
1990 appointment into the alliance of german architects.
foundation of the architectural office mayer bährle in lörrach/baden-württemberg with the goal being to find the correct answer to every new building task, depending on the location, time and space.
the endeavours towards architectural culture were honored with invitations to work, reports and lectures as well as with prizes and awards.
for example: honor award 1991 california council, honor award 1992 american institute of architects, architekturpreis beton 1995, hugo-häring-preis 1991, 1994 and 1997.

1994–98 Gastprofessuren: Harvard University, University of Illinois at Chicago, Columbia University, N.Y.

roland mayer, geboren 1956 in altötting/bayern.
nach der ausbildung als bauzeichner studium der architektur.
in partnerschaft mit günther pfeifer unter anderem realisierung von bauvorhaben mit zaha hadid, frank o. gehry, tadao ando und alvaro siza in weil am rhein, mit frank o. gehry in basel (ch).
1990 berufung in den bund deutscher architekten.
gründung des architekturbüros mayer bährle in lörrach/baden-württemberg mit dem ziel, die richtige antwort für jede neue bauaufgabe zu finden, abhängig von ort, zeit und raum.
das bemühen um die baukultur wurde mit einladungen zu werkberichten und vorträgen sowie mit preisen und auszeichnungen gewürdigt.
z.b. honor award 1991 california council, honor award 1992 american institut of architects, architekturpreis beton 1995, hugo-häring-preis 1991, 1994 und 1997.

peter maximilian bährle, geboren am 01. märz 1955 in zell im wiesental, einem von der textilindustrie geprägten ort im südschwarzwald, und dort seit über zwanzig jahren mit seiner familie wohnhaft.
im anschluß an abitur und militärdienstzeit studium der architektur an der universität karlsruhe.

peter maximilian bährle, born 01 March 1955 in zell/wiesental, a town in the south of the black forest characterized by the textile industry; he has lived there with his family for over twenty years.
after graduating from college and serving in the military, he studied architecture at karlsruhe university. after his diploma, collaboration with günther pfeifer and roland mayer.
in 1993, together with roland mayer, he founded the architectural partnership mayer bährle, based on the principle of understanding the work process, together with everybody involved in the construction, as a patient search for solutions appropriate to each location, time and task. Special importance is given to high-quality materials and a careful execution of the details.

Markus Dochantschi, born 1968 in Neuburg/Danube.
Studied architecture in Darmstadt, collaboration in the office Arata Isozaki & Associates as well as Fumihiko Maki, Tokyo. Since 1995, collaboration in the office Zaha M. Hadid.
Scholarship holder of Carl Duisberg Gesellschaft (1992), as well as the German Academic Exchange Service (1993).

nach dem diplom mitarbeit bei günther pfeifer und roland mayer.
1993 mit roland mayer gründung der architektenpartnerschaft mayer bährle, basierend auf dem grundsatz, den arbeitsprozess zusammen mit allen am bauen beteiligten als geduldige suche nach lösungen zu sehen, welche dem jeweiligen ort, der zeit und der aufgabe angemessen sind, wobei besonderer wert auf qualitätsvolles material und eine sorgfältige detailausführung gelegt wird.

Markus Dochantschi, geboren 1968 in Neuburg an der Donau.
Architekturstudium im Darmstadt. Mitarbeit im Büro Arata Isozaki & Associates, sowie Fumihiko Maki, Tokyo. Seit 1995 Mitarbeit im Büro Zaha M. Hadid.
Stipendiat der Carl Duisberg Gesellschaft (1992), sowie des Deutschen Akademischen Austauschdienstes (1993).

Project Data / Projektdaten

Project
Projekt
Meeting Point Baden-Württemberg/Trinational Environmental Center Gardening Show in Weil am Rhein
Treffpunkt Baden-Württemberg/Trinationales Umweltzentrum Landesgartenschau in Weil am Rhein

Client
Bauherr
Landesgartenschau Weil am Rhein 1999 GmbH
By order of the city of Weil am Rhein
Landesgartenschau Weil am Rhein 1999 GmbH
Im Auftrag der Stadt Weil am Rhein

Architects
Architekten
Zaha Hadid with Schumacher, mayer bährle

Project Architect
Projekt Architekt
Markus Dochantschi

Project Team
Projekt Team
Oliver Domeisen, Wassim Halabi, Garin O'Avazian, Barbara Pfenningsdorf, James Lim

Models
Modelle
June Tamura, Jim Heverin, Jon Richards, Ademir Volic

Construction Management
Projektsteuerung
Büro Fleig Harbauer, Emmendingen

Client Representative
Bauherrenpräsenz
Jürgen Hitze, Stadtbauamt Weil am Rhein

Structural Engineers
Tragwerksplanung
Dr. Ing. L. Martino, Grenzach-Wyhlen / Turin

Electrical and Sanitary Engineers
Elekro-, Sanitärplanung
Küttenbaum Energietechnik, Lörrach

Heating and Ventilation Engineers
Heizungs-und Lüftungsplanung
Delzer Kybernetik, Lörrach

Acoustics Akustik	Ehrsam und Pannach, Lörrach
Survey Vermessung	Stadtbauamt, Stadt Weil am Rhein
Planning and Realization Planung und Ausführung	12/1996–1/1999
Gross Floor Area Bruttogeschoßfläche	845 m^2
Total Cubical Mass Gesamtkubatur	3800 m^3
Total Length Gesamtlänge	140 m
Width Breite	0.85 m–17 m
Height Höhe	0.60 m–6.30 m

Illustration Credits / Bildnachweis

Paintings, models, sketches photographed by /
Paintings, Modelle, Skizzen photographiert von   Edward Woodman

Aerial photo / Luftaufnahme (8)   Rolf Frei

Sketch / Skizze (14)   Dieter Kienast

Aerial photo / Luftaufnahme (39)   Erich Meyer

Cover, Photos / Umschlag, Photos (87–103)   Christian Richters

All other illustrations were supplied by Office Zaha Hadid and mayer bährle.
Alle anderen Abbildungen wurden vom Office Zaha Hadid und mayer bährle zu Verfügung gestellt.